"Michael is the living expression of [obscured by barcode] want to know him, read his book. [obscured] to experience the Truth as it has been revealed to him, step into these pages. You will be embraced by a humble and knowing heart. A timeless and expansive wisdom awaits you."

> —**Bruce Joel Rubin**, Academy Award–winning screenwriter of *Ghost, Jacob's Ladder, My Life, Deep Impact, Stuart Little 2, The Last Mimzy,* and *The Time Traveler's Wife*

"*Boundless Awareness* is a delight to read, as it invites the reader to embody the 'loving awareness' you are reading about with alive metaphors and heart-centered guided meditations. Michael addresses important topics such as boundless awareness versus the intimacy of experience, sudden versus gradual awakening, nothing to be done versus something to be done, no practice versus practice, and transpersonal versus personal in a way that is down-to-earth and a breath of fresh air."

> —**Loch Kelly**, author of *Shift Into Freedom*

"Michael A. Rodriguez brings the words of a poet, the keen eye of a scholar, and the heart of a devotee of truth to this skillful evocation of non-dual realization. He covers the territory thoroughly, including the subtleties of embodying our inherent perfection in these imperfect human forms. An excellent resource for beginners and seasoned seekers alike."

> —**Stephan Bodian**, founder and teacher at the School for Awakening, and author of *Wake Up Now* and *Beyond Mindfulness*

"In the growing field of non-dual literature, *Boundless Awareness* shines with an unusual clarity, warmth, creativity, and nuanced insight. Michael also breaks new ground with his discussion of post-awakening shadow integration, deftly including truths from both direct and progressive spiritual approaches. This is cutting-edge work: engaging, inspiring, and beautifully written. I highly recommend it!"

> —**John J. Prendergast, PhD**, retired adjunct professor of psychology at the California Institute of Integral Studies, and author of *In Touch*

"With incredible clarity and an unbounded heart, Michael masterfully guides you to step out of the prison of thought-created experience and into the freedom of an undivided view, in which the shining essence of reality reveals itself. A beautifully eloquent book that will undoubtedly serve to untangle many of the preconceptions about the 'awakened state' and provide helpful pointers and practices to those willing to embark on the journey of direct realization."

> —**Amoda Maa,** author of *Embodied Enlightenment*

"Michael delivers grounded, translucent teachings that penetrate and liberate both mind and heart. His book is a sublime manual for awakening, and it delivers much-needed clarity and precision on the liberating process of removing that which obscures our true nature. There is a clear and radiant transmission inherent within these pages. May it land and take root in your heart."

> —**Susanne Marie,** spiritual teacher, speaker, and group facilitator of Life Living Itself

"I have read many spiritual books over the ten years I have been interviewing people for www.conscious.tv, but I found that Michael's book has an exceptional clarity that gave me a deeper understanding of who we really are."

—**Renate McNay**, www.conscious.tv

"As someone who quickly became a close friend, and in three appearances on *Buddha at the Gas Pump*, I've found Michael to possess a rare blend of clarity, wisdom, and humanness. Those qualities come through clearly in this book."

—**Rick Archer**, founder and host of *Buddha at the Gas Pump*

"Skillfully drawing from both direct and progressive path practices, Michael has given us an integrative manual for awakening. His intellectual sensitivity and openhearted ease shine through in these pages. I sincerely hope that *Boundless Awareness* finds the wide readership it deserves—it is one of the most lucid, helpful, and accomplished books that I have read on this subject in recent years."

—**Julian Noyce**, founder of Non-Duality Press

BOUNDLESS AWARENESS

A LOVING PATH TO SPIRITUAL AWAKENING AND FREEDOM FROM SUFFERING

MICHAEL A. RODRIGUEZ

NON-DUALITY PRESS
An Imprint of New Harbinger Publications

Publisher's Note

This publication is designed to provide accurate and authoritative information in regard to the subject matter covered. It is sold with the understanding that the publisher is not engaged in rendering psychological, financial, legal, or other professional services. If expert assistance or counseling is needed, the services of a competent professional should be sought.

Distributed in Canada by Raincoast Books

Copyright © 2018 by Michael A. Rodriguez
Non-Duality Press
An imprint of New Harbinger Publications, Inc.
5674 Shattuck Avenue
Oakland, CA 94609
www.newharbinger.com

Cover design by Amy Shoup

Edited by Gretel Hakanson

All Rights Reserved

Library of Congress Cataloging-in-Publication Data on file

20   19   18

10   9   8   7   6   5   4   3   2   1 First Printing

for my mother and father

CONTENTS

FOREWORD

What if you are not a separate person born into a universe made of dead matter? What if everything is vibrantly alive, all of it the expression of One Consciousness? What if you *are* that boundless awareness, unborn and indestructible, in which the whole universe appears and disappears? What if the awakening you are seeking is already fully present, simply unnoticed? If you really saw and felt the truth of these possibilities as your actual present reality, how would that change your life? That's what this book is all about. It's a book that will be helpful to both beginners and to those who have been on the pathless path for many years.

I've known Michael Rodriguez since he was a college student. We met through the work of Toni Packer, who was an important teacher for us both. In the beginning, Michael and I knew each other only through occasional email exchanges. In 2014, after he moved to the Bay Area, we finally met in person, and we quickly became close friends. In our dialogues in these last years, Michael has often been a teacher to me. In the last year, it has brought me great joy to watch him make the leap into being available as a teacher to the wider world.

Michael sees and writes with clarity and sensitivity. He brings both an open heart and an intellectual acuity to the table, but above all, he brings the fruits of his own direct inquiry, exploration, and discovery—dissolving into and abiding as boundless awareness. It is that kind of direct exploration and abidance in the Heart that Michael encourages others to take up. He offers guided meditations and exercises throughout this book—"visceral somatic practices" as he calls them—that allow you to directly experience what is being pointed out in the text so that your understanding never stops at the intellectual or cognitive level, but is always brought deeper into the aliveness and immediacy of non-conceptual presence and direct realization.

Michael offers an integrated approach to awakening that is, in his words, "at once transcendent *and* imminent, awake *and* embodied, transpersonal *and* personal, divine *and* human." He recognizes and honors both the timeless absolute truth of what has never been absent and also the relative truth of the unending evolutionary journey of discovery and integration that occurs over time. His expression marries the path of negation (or detachment) and the path of inclusion (or love), illuminating both the emptiness and the fullness, the oneness and the uniqueness of everything. Michael uses language skillfully, but points beyond language to an emptying out where all concepts are left behind, even the subtlest and most sublime.

Unlike some contemporary non-dualists, Michael does not gloss over or try to glibly bypass the painful patterns of self-contraction that tend to reappear even after an initial awakening, patterns that pull consciousness back into suffering and identification as a separate self. But very importantly, Michael roots this "shadow work" in the recognition of what is always whole and complete, rather than approaching it from the limited perspective of the psychological self and then trying to fix that illusory phantom.

Michael has a wonderfully rich and eclectic sensibility, and he brings a fierce and passionate intensity, energy, and devotion to whatever he does. That passion and devotion are beautifully manifested in this book. There is pure love in these pages, pure light. Michael is a natural teacher with years of teaching experience that have honed the skills needed to communicate and share his discoveries. I can only imagine that his expression will continue to evolve and flourish in the years to come.

I have found Michael to be unpretentious, genuine, down-to-earth, full of heart, and open to looking freshly and seeing new things. He is totally dedicated to sharing awakening. He offers the essential wisdom of non-duality in clean, clear language, without the often-distracting whistles, bells, dogmas, and roles of tradition.

This is a book that can change your life and take you on a journey from suffering to freedom. Enjoy it, savor it, soak in it, work with it, contemplate it. May it invite you to dissolve into the boundless awareness from which Michael speaks and to which he so clearly and directly points.

—Joan Tollifson is the author of *Bare-Bones Meditation, Awake in the Heartland, Painting the Sidewalk with Water,* and *Nothing to Grasp.*

ACKNOWLEDGMENTS

I was blessed to have two extraordinary parents with boundless hearts. My father was remarkably tenderhearted, humble, warm, and sensitive, and my mother is the most naturally thoughtful, sensitive, nurturing, compassionate being I have ever met. She has unconditionally loved and supported me every step of the way. It is impossible for me to convey the depth of my gratitude for the countless sacrifices both of them made on my behalf, without which nothing would have been possible for me. I bow to them with the utmost respect and reverence, and I dedicate this book to them.

I would also like to acknowledge Ty Anderson and Ernie Williams, two quirky philosophy professors who first introduced me to the wisdom of the East when I was in college and who subsequently became dear friends. In addition to being first-rate teachers, they were my greatest early spiritual guides, mentors, and benefactors. This book would not have been possible without the immense generosity of spirit that they displayed and the extraordinary grace that I received through them.

Thank you to Nisargadatta Maharaj for his extraordinary clarity and insight into the nature of reality. He is my greatest foundational teacher. He has become so much a part of me that I echo his words, either consciously or unconsciously, throughout this book. That is also true of two other teachers, Mooji and Rupert Spira, whose differences perfectly complemented each other for me and whose teachings Nisargadatta had prepared me to receive.

Although I had been well prepared for the ultimate realization of the "path of negation," which I discuss in chapters 5 and 6, it was not until I encountered Mooji's teachings that I was emptied in an absolute sense. I'm especially grateful for his supremely skillful ability to expose subtle strategies of mind and to point away from all experience toward pure awareness. He also touched my heart very deeply, woke me up to the natural joy of being, opened the wellspring of intuition and spontaneity, and inspired me profoundly. He had a monumental impact both on me and on this book, and I am grateful to him beyond measure.

While Mooji helped empty me out, Rupert helped fill me back up. Rupert also had a monumental influence on my understanding, experience, and articulation of true nature, especially in regard to the "path of inclusion." Prior to meeting Rupert, I had deeply meditated not only on the "direct path" teachings, including those by Atmananda Krishna Menon, but also on all the classic spiritual texts in the Kashmir Shaivist tradition emphasizing the "tantric" (i.e., energetic) aspect of consciousness. But it was not until I encountered Rupert's teaching that I became awakened to the fact that all experience arises in and is made out of consciousness. Since this book is largely devoted to displacing the conventional "matter model" of experience and awakening the reader to the seamlessness and aliveness of consciousness that Rupert awakened in me—a form of knowing that he calls a "feeling-understanding"—it is fair to say that he had the greatest influence on this book as a whole (although I do have a markedly different way of speaking about the "path of negation"). I often draw from Rupert's vocabulary and lines of reasoning; in fact, I have so absorbed his tantric style into my own DNA that many of the pointers and guided meditations in this book bear the genetic imprint of his overall approach. In addition to liberating consciousness from its imagined limitations and establishing the vibrancy of experience, Rupert also spoke deeply to my heart and gave me many of the tools to integrate my awakening. I am grateful beyond words for his exquisite guidance, beautiful presence, and warm friendship.

I initially met Joan Tollifson through her writing; I had read her first book *Bare-Bones Meditation* when I was in college and then briefly had contact with her while she was working at Springwater Center. Over time, we got to know each other well, and I'm now honored to call her one of my closest friends. Joan was also an important teacher to me in many ways. She's exceptionally insightful, down-to-earth, unpretentious, and true. She's also a superb writer against whose sentences I measured my own. In fact, some of the insights in this book were inspired by my encounters with Joan's writing or by my discussions with her. I would also like to acknowledge her for being the strongest supporter of my own work as a spiritual teacher and for writing the beautiful foreword to this book, for which I am deeply and most humbly grateful.

I have had too many teachers and influences to name all of them. However, I would like specifically to acknowledge and thank several more who were pivotal: Shankara, Huang Po, Ramana Maharshi, Carl Jung, Alan Watts, Joseph Campbell, Robert Adams, J. Krishnamurti, Toni Packer, Pir Vilayat Inayat Khan, Thich Nhat Hanh, Jack Kornfield, and Fr. Curtis Almquist. These teachers played a significant role on my "pathless path," and I thank all of them for their remarkable gifts and blessings.

A very warm thank you from the bottom of my heart to Julian and Catherine Noyce at Non-Duality Press for believing in this book, for being patient enough to wait for the right time to move forward with it, and for originally pitching it to the folks at New Harbinger Publications. Julian and Catherine have been remarkably kind, supportive, and generous. I am deeply grateful to them and honored to call them friends.

I would like to thank the entire team at New Harbinger Publications; I could not have asked for a better publishing experience. Thank you especially to my remarkable team of editors whose feedback helped me improve the book tremendously. The editorial manager, Clancy Drake; my developmental editor, Jennifer Holder; and my copyeditor, Gretel Hakanson, were indispensable. All of them helped me transform and shape the book into what it has become.

It is to Camille Hayes, my acquisitions editor at New Harbinger, that I owe the biggest debt of gratitude. Camille's highly encouraging response to the initial manuscript, coupled with her prescient vision for the book and constant enthusiastic support, inspired me to produce my best possible writing. This book is incomparably better under her guidance than it would otherwise have been. Her sparkling intelligence, cognitive strength, and deep sensitivity made working with her a joy and an honor.

INTRODUCTION

We are living in an age of scientific materialism in which people are spiritually parched. Ours is largely a culture of material excess and spiritual impoverishment. It is dominated by an increasingly unhealthy reliance on alienating and dehumanizing modes of technology. As I work with others in private sessions and in groups, it is clear that many people are genuinely searching for deeper, more spiritually nourishing registers of knowledge and experience. Some are even searching for spiritual awakening and for the end of the search itself.

My own heart has deepened profoundly as I have had the honor of hearing firsthand about people's suffering, as they express it to me in a way that they would not normally do with anyone else. The unconditional love, nurturing presence, and total safety of our individual and collective meetings provide people with a rare opportunity to tell the truth about how they feel—and to hear the truth about their infinite potential. You may also experience a version of what people report to me on a regular basis.

For example, you may have been guided and prompted to read this book because you are suffering from the psychological or emotional pain associated with feeling regretful, depressed, anxious, lonely, or fearful. Perhaps you have the nagging feeling that you are lacking something essential, that you missed the boat or haven't fulfilled your potential. Perhaps U2's "I Still Haven't Found What I'm Looking For" or Colin Hay's "Waiting for My Real Life to Begin" is your theme song. Perhaps you feel as though there's more to life than working in a job you don't enjoy, making money to pay the bills, buying ever more material things, and saving for a retirement you may never reach. Perhaps you just want to feel at peace and comfortable in your own skin, to feel alive, to feel less existentially anguished, to feel loved and lovable, or to relate to yourself and others with openness and kindness. Perhaps you are seeking clarity about the nature of existence, about why humanity is in the dire state that it's in, about what lies beyond your biographical identity and persona, about the nature of life and consciousness, about the true meaning of love, or about why you're "not there yet" despite having been on the spiritual path for years or decades.

These are universal human concerns. To resolve any of them, you will need experiential insight into your true nature. When you inquire into your true nature through the lens of wisdom, you will come to see that all your confusion and discontent constellates around a false self that does not actually exist—or that exists relative to a deeper, more authentic self that is the true source of the timeless peace and contentment for which your heart longs. This source abides here and now if only you could be guided to see it in all its simplicity. This book is meant to guide you in that direction by addressing the core issue of false self-identification, not from the perspective of traditional "self-help," which often substantiates the false self that resides at the center of seeking, but from the perspective of a radically different sense of self that goes altogether beyond your conventional personal identity and limiting belief structures.

You are Already Boundless and Free

The main claim of this book is that you are already boundless and free and that the entire misunderstanding of your true nature rests on a colossal yet simple error of limited self-identification; this error is rooted in the conceptual realm and becomes substantiated at the feeling level with minor to acute self-contractions in the forms of mental, emotional, and muscular tensions. These habitual self-contractions are responsible for driving the majority of humanity's frustrated behavior. Most people normally identify with the limited objects of their experience instead of investigating the actual subject (or self) of everything that they experience. They particularly identify with the self-contracted "body-mind," a term I use to denote your entire psychosomatic identity, which you will come to see as objectively observable. When you soften your body-mind, investigate your self closely, and empty it of absolutely everything you have learned, you discover that it is not objectively observable and that it does not have any limits; it is, in fact, "uncreated," meaning that the core of your being never actually came into existence and is consequently beyond birth and death. It was only ever the conceptual misidentification of your self with the body-mind as an apparently separate object that caused an unnatural division between "inner" and "outer" experience and a resultant irritation that we call "suffering." Simply put, as long as you feel limited and separate, you are bound to suffer and to cause suffering.

What Is Non-Duality and Awakening?

If you are reading this book, chances are that you are already aware of and in touch with a more authentic reality beneath the facade of your conditioned personality and are longing to deepen your knowledge and experience of it. You are probably at least partly if not wholly committed to "waking up" from the nightmare of seeking whatever you feel you lack. On the other hand, you may be new to this topic and feel an inexplicable hunger to know something deeper. In either case, I warmly welcome you. This book contains everything you potentially need in order to awaken spiritually and to live a life free from suffering. Together, we will go on a mental, emotional, somatic, and intuitive journey into the heart of reality, which is essentially non-dual. "Non-duality" refers to the undivided nature of existence. The original word in Sanskrit is *advaita*, which literally means "not two" or "without duality." Non-duality as a spiritual path teaches that there's only one reality (not two different realities) out of which all experience is made—in other words, that you and the universe are made of a single source-substance. The most common terms in non-dual literature for that unitary substance are "consciousness" and "awareness," both of which I use synonymously throughout this book (despite their subtle shades of meaning in different contexts). Duality or "twoness," on the other hand, implies that you are conscious (one subtle substance) and that the world is made of unconscious matter (a second gross substance). This dualistic misinterpretation makes you feel painfully, unnaturally separate from and at odds with an inert world made of material components that are apparently "other" than you. It degrades what is in fact radiant, conscious spirit to inanimate and unintelligent material components that lack meaning or purpose. When you view the world as material and other, you will either desire or fear the objects of your experience.

However, when you investigate life closely with the singular eye of wisdom, you discover the following:

- In reality, there is nothing missing, lacking, or wrong.

- There are no sharp dividing lines anywhere in nature, only harmonious interdependence with no absolute beginning or end.

- Rather than being a static product, your body-mind is an energetic process that's braided with the limitless environment.

- Awareness is a boundless, vibrant principle of aliveness out of which all experience is made.

- You are boundless and free in your essential being.

The experiential insight into these truths could be called "awakening," "enlightenment," or "self-realization." You literally "wake up" to your infinite and eternal nature and dis-cover your non-separation from all of life rather than sleepwalking through your days as a separate island of identity. To use the old analogy, you realize that you are the formless current of electricity rather than a separate light-bulb with its own source of light. I refer to awakening as a "dis-covery" to emphasize the fact that awakening fundamentally entails un-covering your inherent wholeness rather than adding something new onto yourself.

In order to lead you into a firsthand realization of your essential wholeness and freedom, thereby eradicating or at least reducing the suffering associated with feeling otherwise, this book follows a methodical trajectory that could be summarized broadly as a process of deconstruction, reconstruction, and integration. Throughout this journey, the pointers in each chapter will help you systematically abolish the imaginary division between "inner" and "outer" experience and remove the irritating sense of psychological self-consciousness while retaining the healthy sense of self-awareness, leaving you in the natural state of "empty fullness."

My Spiritual Journey in a Nutshell

Although my own spiritual path was not at all linear in the way I have laid out the following chapters, I modeled this book largely on the broad outline of my own spiritual trajectory, giving shape and form to what was in fact a long, winding journey. I was initially an academic, having earned three postgraduate degrees and then having taught various humanistic subjects at the university level for over a decade. Academia in general and teaching in particular were for a while a great joy. My passion for literature, art, and music was connected to my passion for the spiritual path. I always tried to instill in my students an appreciation for the sanctity of beauty. Ever since I was young, it was my experience that beauty and truth were intimately related. Beauty, in fact, is the creative expression of truth; it awakens us to our divine nature by dissolving the separate sense of self, making us transparent to the truth of our boundless being, and filling us with aliveness, joy, gratitude, awe, and wonder. Everything I taught always came back to the theme of spiritual awakening because that's what really mattered to me.

Eventually, however, I became disenchanted with the suffocating demands of mainstream academia, didn't want to be constrained by teaching any longer in the traditional university setting, and wanted to drop down from the head to the heart on a full-time basis. I basically wanted to devote my entire life to spiritual awakening, a process that had begun well over two decades earlier and had even included living in a monastery for two years, an experience that allowed me to deepen my innate love of silence, solitude, and contemplation.

In fact, my earliest spiritual contemplation arose spontaneously when I was around seven or eight years old. As I was getting ready for school one morning, I started to ponder a conundrum. For some reason that I can no longer remember, I was thinking about the vastness of the physical universe and began wondering what lay on the other side when you got to the end of it. I remember being awestruck by the question, straining with all my might to figure it out. My mind kept bumping up against itself as it tried to imagine that unimaginable scenario. In retrospect, I was essentially meditating on a Zen "koan," although I had no idea what that meant at the time. I now see that contemplation as a karmic seed that eventually grew into my spiritual quest and then flowered into the book you are now reading. In fact, this book represents an answer to that very conundrum I was destined to ask myself all those years ago. Interestingly, the work I do now directly addresses this question and offers what is for me the definitive answer—not from a conventional perspective but from the perspective of boundless awareness.

As I suggested above, my spiritual path was for many years intertwined with my academic journey. When I was exposed to the wisdom of the East in my undergraduate courses, I sought out many spiritual guides in many traditions and read voraciously, which eventually led me to Harvard Divinity School where I earned a master's degree in theology with an emphasis in comparative religion. The most significant early spiritual experiences I had were with Roshi Philip Kapleau, with whom I began attending Zen retreats when I was a teenager. The first time I walked into a zendo (a traditional meditational hall in the Zen tradition), I felt immediately at home. Although he was old and physically ailing at that time, Roshi Kapleau had a powerful, commanding presence that touched me deeply. Soon after meeting Roshi Kapleau, Toni Packer, who was his initial dharma heir, became my primary spiritual teacher in upstate New York. Being with her was remarkably formative, partly because I was so young and receptive. She had a beautiful, spacious way of looking freshly at whatever arose and a refreshingly non-dogmatic, non-hierarchical approach to awakening, all of which resonated with me. She was passionate and even rhapsodic during her talks, which had a tendency to trigger deep insights into the nature of reality.

At the end of one retreat, Toni read excerpts from Nisargadatta Maharaj's *I Am That*, which turned out to be a major turning point; that book quickly became the most important teacher in my life and set the foundation for everything that was to unfold. Nisargadatta cut right through all the dogma and ritual and pointed directly to my inherent freedom in a way that felt totally familiar and resonant with the deepest recesses of my being.

During this early period, I also steeped myself in Carl Jung's collected works; Jung taught me a great deal about consciousness, the process of individuation, and shadow integration. He was an incredibly soulful teacher who spoke to the immense mystery, creativity, and beauty of my humanity. To this day, I am "Jung at heart."

When I eventually left my academic teaching post, I took a leap into the unknown and fully immersed myself in many spiritual teachings but particularly those by Mooji and Rupert Spira. I ate, drank, breathed, lived, and slept non-duality—literally! Something was struggling to be born—or to be *unborn*, as it were. Based on my exposure to these (and many other) extraordinary teachers, I went through a five-year period of purification and alchemical transmutation where my body-mind was being emptied out, awakened, and integrated in the ways that I describe in this book.

Rather than making me "special," awakening actually has the opposite effect precisely because it's transpersonal, which is why "I" language can be so tricky and even misleading. Rather than being self-aggrandizing, genuine awakening is the essence of humility since it reveals the fact that we're all identical in essence and that, in reality, no one is more or less "special" or "spiritual" than anyone else. My life is now dedicated to being of service for the sheer joy of sharing the realizations that I offer in this book and helping people discover for themselves the truth that they are already undivided and whole. I have come to see that loving service and heartfelt sharing are the meaning and purpose of life.

Although I am grateful to all my teachers in a relative sense, I now see them—in fact, all *experience*—as aspects of myself within myself. Awareness plants wisdom seeds inside its own being and then draws to itself the necessary nutrients apparently from the "outside" in order to activate the encoded potential of those seeds, allowing them to sprout and grow and flourish according to their destiny. Once a wisdom seed is planted, it will bear fruit sooner or later if you provide the key nutrients of earnest interest and loving attention. I can now see how everything I have done has been a variation on the theme of this book. If you reflect on your life, you will begin to discern your own themes or motifs that have formed the backbone of your individual path. Your natural joys and resonances are expressions of the encoded seeds of your potential and destiny, primarily because you did not "choose" them; you simply dis-cover them without knowing why they are there and then, if you have faith in yourself, water them without knowing exactly how or when they will flower. Whatever they are, awareness has planted those wisdom seeds inside your being in order to unfold its deepest potential in your unique lifestream. As you will discover the more you awaken, awareness gives you the intuitive sensitivity to discern the synchronistic clues that life provides you out of sheer grace and the inspiration to explore them in the spirit of high adventure.

The Spiritual Background of This Book

Throughout this book, I have largely avoided using fancy theological jargon or direct quotations from other sources, inserting only a handful of them and primarily relying, instead, on my own firsthand experience. However, this book does represent a distillation of the deepest knowledge of the ancient wisdom traditions from which I have drawn in a general sense, particularly those from India (Advaita Vedanta and Buddhism), Kashmir (Shaivism), Tibet (Dzogchen and Mahamudra), China (Taoism and Chan), and Japan (Zen). I also draw from mystical Christianity. At the same time, this book does not fit into or espouse any tradition or path. It is inclusive of and ultimately transcends all paths that lead toward a recognition of the essentially undivided nature of reality. I hope that the teachings in this book complement rather than threaten whatever your path may be. Consequently, although my approach is deeply rooted in non-duality and some Jungian depth psychology, you can have any religious, spiritual, or therapeutic affiliation—or none at all—in order to engage this work.

It is important to know that these teachings are part of an ancient heritage, that they have been "time tested" over thousands of years. They might seem new or revolutionary only in the sense that they're unfamiliar to most people in the West for cultural reasons, but you actually know what I'm pointing to so directly that you may have overlooked these simple truths, living instead within a conditioned framework of painful duality that has become "normalized." You have simply acquired habitual ways of thinking and feeling limited, bound, and separate that were not original to you.

How to Read This Book

This book may offer a markedly different kind of reading experience than other books you may have read, so I would like to offer six suggestions about how you might approach the text. It is my hope that these suggestions will give you a context and orientation to help you navigate the book effectively and gain the maximum benefit from it.

Read the Book Sequentially

Although you could dip into this book randomly and still get some benefit, I highly suggest that you read it sequentially from beginning to end without skipping anything because the book systematically builds toward deeper and deeper levels of experiential insight and embodied understanding. I would also suggest that you consider rereading it, as there are many early points that will come to life only after you have completed the book. There's also some repetition and overlap throughout the book, but they are meant to drive home certain points over and over again. I will also sometimes make the same point but in a different context, hopefully shedding light on it from another perspective.

Your Felt Experience Is the Key

Despite the fact that I often use logic to deconstruct the false conceptual reality in which most people live, which sometimes results in a rational tone, this book is not "philosophical" in the sense of being theoretical, abstract, or speculative. It is meant to be experiential, full-bodied, and heart-centered. Although it is important to address the mental level and put the mind's doubts to rest, the most important thing is to open your system to a somatic resonance with the truth of your own being so you have *a felt sense* of wholeness and interconnectivity rather than a merely intellectual or cognitive understanding.

To emphasize this point, I use a coaching paradigm with simple guided meditations and exercises woven throughout the book to make the material, which can be conceptually challenging, more approachable, down-to-earth, and practical. Since most suffering originates at a subtle sensational level, the guided meditations and exercises will help bring about a kinesthetic state of relaxed openness so you are more likely to notice and appreciate the sheer wonder and incandescent radiance of awareness. I employ not only logic, therefore, but also visceral somatic practices to help you immediately embody and express your awakening at a more intuitive level beyond the realm of language and concepts. I'm simply describing the fruit; actually tasting it is up to you. For this reason, the guided meditations and exercises are the juicy part.

Read the Book Meditatively

Many of the sentences you are about to read are dense, layered, interwoven, and meditative, potentially lending themselves both to immediate shifts in understanding and to slow dissolves of old limiting patterns that no longer serve you. In order to deepen your meditative experience of this book, you might consider approaching it in the Christian contemplative tradition of *lectio divina*, which means "divine reading." *Lectio divina* is a style of encountering a text that promotes union with whatever term you might use to denote the highest mystery: "awareness," "consciousness," "a higher power," "God," "presence," "nature," or "life." It is helpful first to prepare the ground for engaging in *lectio divina* by inviting a calm and tranquil state, which can simply be done by taking a few deep breaths, relaxing the body-mind, and dropping down into the felt sense of being with "loving awareness," a beautiful phrase that I borrow from Saint John of the Cross and use throughout this book. I will often invite you into this state at the beginning of a guided meditation or exercise, but you might consider doing so before you pick up the book each time. The point is to read and contemplate the text in a relaxed mood of open receptivity with love of truth as your motivation.

In order to encourage a slower, more meditative reading pace, I have buffered the paragraphs with subject headings, with italicized sentences, and with standout sentences that consist of brief statements separated from the rest of the text for emphasis. Think of them as speed bumps. Rather than speeding through the text, take your time. It is my hope that breaking up the material in these ways will make the material easier to absorb. So after reaching the end of a section, a sentence that I have italicized, or a standout sentence that I have inserted to catch your attention, I invite you to meditate on what you have read, especially when something resonates with you. If the cells in your body vibrate with a pleasant sensation, an "aha" recognition, or even a simple "huh," that's an indication that what you read either aligns with truth or at least warrants further contemplation. It's helpful to stop reading at these times, to put the book down, to allow your cells to absorb the vibrational resonance fully, and to rewire accordingly. Hang out there for at least a few minutes. The realization of your wholeness should result in a deep cellular relaxation that allows your system to become flowingly integrated at a systemic level, thereby triggering and fostering the innate healing capacity of the body. Don't rush this contemplative, nurturing process; while certain insights might be sudden, truth-absorption, healing, and neural rewiring take time.

Live the Meditations and Exercises Joyfully

Since the guided meditations and exercises in this book really are the heart of the matter, giving you a chance to put into immediate practice the concepts you have just learned, I encourage you to think of the guided meditations and exercises not as one-time events but as *a way of life* so there's no difference between the meditation cushion and daily life. Ideally the integration of your wisdom with your day-to-day life will be seamless. Unlike books that feed you static information, this book requires your active and earnest participation not only in terms of grokking the concepts, but also and most importantly in terms of performing the meditations throughout your day in a spirit of joyful exploration. Discovering your true nature, which is synonymous with peace, should be a *pleasure*. In the words of the Buddha, the path of awakening is "lovely in the beginning, lovely in the middle, and lovely in the end."

Try to Cultivate a Don't-Know Mind

I've done my best to express the message of spiritual awakening as clearly as possible, but since words are inherently dualistic, they are incapable of expressing reality with absolute accuracy. At best, therefore, anything I write is only approximately true. In a sense, reality is simply what remains when thought falls silent. All the words in this book are straining to point to that simple silence. Since no statement about reality can have absolute truth, you must ultimately come to "unlearn" everything you think you know. This process of unlearning first entails becoming aware that you are identified with relative knowledge, inherited beliefs, and unexamined assumptions. You can then loosen your grip on them and begin to empty them out as an act of loving devotion toward your deepest and truest self.

Cultivating what Zen calls a "don't-know mind" turns out to have an incredibly healthy effect because it keeps you fresh and humble, empty and serviceable. While this book frames experience within the wisdom traditions that I listed above, you must be willing to live outside any frame of reference—even a "non-dual" frame such as this one. Otherwise, you run the risk of becoming reductionist, fundamentalist, or evangelical, living within yet another prison of a new set of ideas. There's a saying in Zen: "If you see the Buddha, kill the Buddha." The point isn't to adopt non-duality as a philosophy but to live free of all philosophies and conceptual molds, all of which are prisons. Once the pointers in this book have done their work, mainly of erasing the irritating and alienating sense of self-consciousness that makes you feel separate from the world, you forget them so you can live naturally, spontaneously, and integrally again as you did in childhood, but now with the depth and wisdom of a sage.

Don't Get Stuck on the "Pointers"

I use the term "pointer" quite frequently and want to define it clearly so you don't get stuck on things like terminology. There's a famous image in Zen of a master pointing to the moon while the student ignorantly looks at the master's finger instead of at the moon. A pointer is a gesture *toward* truth but is not itself the truth. It's a suggestion to look in a particular direction in order to arrive at the reality to which it's pointing rather than getting fixated on the pointer itself. If you mistake a pointer in this book for what it's pointing to, you will be like the student looking at the Zen master's finger instead of at the moon of truth.

The Importance of Being Earnest

You might have noticed that I used the word "earnest" twice in this introduction; I also use it throughout the book. The importance of being earnest cannot be overstated. I borrow the word *earnestness* from Nisargadatta Maharaj, who uses it in *I Am That* perhaps more than any other word. Earnestness, which means honesty or sincerity with oneself, is vital because without it, you will lack clarity of purpose and may even sabotage yourself on the spiritual path. I often ask my clients during the first meeting what their heart wants above all things. I ask them, "What is your heart's deepest longing?" When I stress the importance of being honest with themselves, they usually pause for a long time, scanning their heart for the answer. They often end up saying that truth or freedom is their heart's deepest longing, in which case we can truly begin. Without that clarity, the desire for other relative things will siphon much of the "earnest interest" and "loving attention" that I listed above as the key nutrients for the wisdom seeds that were planted in you.

As you embark on the journey of reading and engaging with this book, you may want to take a moment to ask yourself what your heart wants more than anything. That clarity will help orient you accordingly.

CHAPTER 1

THE MISERY OF SEEKING

Woody Allen's *Annie Hall* is one of my all-time favorite movies. The scene that gets me every time is when Woody's character, Alvy Singer, is in a bookstore with Diane Keaton's eponymous character. Alvy and Annie are just getting to know each other, so Alvy picks up two books about death and suggests that she read them. He confesses to being obsessed with death and to being a pessimist. He then tells her that if they're going to be a couple, she should know that he divides everyone into one of two categories: "the horrible" and "the miserable." The first category, "the horrible," includes people who have physical disabilities, such as blindness, and people who are terminally ill. The other category, "the miserable," consists of everyone else. "So when you go through life," Alvy says to Annie, "you should be thankful that you're miserable because you're very lucky to *be* miserable."

Although it's an incredibly funny line, there's a lot of truth in it. Whether people know it or not, misery characterizes the "normal" state of human consciousness because it consists of endless cycles of dissatisfaction, restlessness, and discontent. It's dominated by insatiable desire and chronic fear. It's a zombie state where your natural aliveness becomes deadened and your inherent peace and freedom seem to become eclipsed. It is the "normal" state for most humans who are "lucky" enough not to be worse off, but it is certainly not natural or healthy.

In fact, when you consider the world from a conventional human perspective, you cannot help but feel that something is seriously wrong. The amount of suffering is so incalculably vast and pervasive that any sensitive person can easily feel overwhelmed or even paralyzed by grief and fear. Even so-called "normal" and "well-adjusted" people anesthetize themselves in countless ways to cope with the pain of the human condition. Many people seek to suppress the insecurity they feel and to fill the void in their life with meaningless repetitions of experience that merely go on reinforcing the lack they feel. They do anything to avoid feeling the way they do: alienated and adrift in a life of unfulfilling work, empty relationships, and endless consumerism.

The "normal" state of human consciousness could even be described as a "hell realm"—one of the six "bardos" in the Tibetan Buddhist tradition. The bardos technically refer to the transitional realms of experience right after physical death (in Tibetan, "bardo" means "intermediate or transitional state"). However, you could view any transitional state, including those in life, as a bardo characterized by a self-perpetuating process of recycling that looks something like this:

- feeling vaguely or acutely incomplete

- seeking completion in the world of mundane or even spiritual experience

- failing to achieve a sense of completion

- feeling frustrated

- feeling vaguely or acutely incomplete again

This vicious circle has to be recognized objectively in order to break your identification with it. The problem is that we humans create and perpetuate this vicious circle without knowing it; the symptoms of our suffering are so pervasive that they are virtually invisible. Chronic mental, emotional, and somatic pain has come to constitute the "normal" state for most humans, but as you will discover, the "norm" is in fact an altered, abnormal state of consciousness.

Even when people *do* recognize their own cyclic suffering, they are slow to respond and may even actively perpetuate it. Most people are either desensitized or strangely indifferent to their suffering. We in our modern Western culture make an arbitrary distinction between physical pain and mental-emotional suffering, responding to the former and often ignoring the latter. For example, if your shoulder bone popped out of its joint while you were playing a sport, you probably wouldn't suppress or simply tolerate the pain, nor would you hesitate to attend to the injury with your full, undivided attention. You probably wouldn't drink the pain away for years or decades. Pain is the body's way of signaling that something is dis-eased; as we all know instinctively, it's a call for prompt attention. Yet, when it comes to mental and emotional pain, many people *do* ignore or simply tolerate it—sometimes for many years, decades, or even an entire lifetime—instead of treating the mental, emotional, and somatic body as a perfectly tuned biofeedback system that signals when your ways of thinking and feeling are "out of joint" with reality.

Maturity consists of turning the same fullness of mind, or *mindfulness*, that you would devote to your physical body to your thoughts and emotions. It consists of asking certain fundamental questions that have your best interests at heart:

- Why do I suffer?

- What is the cause of suffering?

- Is suffering normal or natural?

- Can I be free of suffering?

- Who is the "I" who suffers, anyway?

These are the kinds of intelligent questions that signal the dawning of mental health, emotional intelligence, wisdom, and liberation. The purpose of this chapter is to shed light on how seeking and attachment to desire cause suffering and to suggest that your natural state is not one of misery but one of timeless peace, contentment, joy, and freedom. I end by stressing the importance of taking the best possible care of yourself so that wellbeing rather than misery becomes your natural default state.

The Mechanics of Desire

Despite all the overwhelming evidence to the contrary, you may still hope that you can find lasting fulfillment in a fleeting world. However, you know deep down that material things cannot deliver lasting fulfillment because they are undependable and ephemeral by nature. They don't last. Dwelling on the past and future, forever pursuing things that you think will (but secretly know will not) bring you lasting peace, creates an endlessly frustrating, futile, self-perpetuating loop. Waking up from this mode of misery requires that you clearly see the inherently painful nature of the habitual pursuit of things that you *think* or *feel* will make you happy and at peace.

Awakening is largely about coming to the conclusion that attachment to desire, the feverish search for something "more," obscures the boundless perfection of things as they are. It also obscures the bounty before you. Desire is actually the movement of misery. Society conditions us to spend our lives insatiably desirous, a state of restlessness and discontent on which consumerism depends. Every time you get a new gadget, for example, it quickly becomes outdated and replaced by a new generation of technology. But when you wise up, you come to understand that nothing created can truly satisfy your hunger or address your misery at the root except waking up from the dream of incompletion and lack. Almost everyone turns a blind eye to this simple truth and seeks to build permanent happiness with temporary materials—an altogether unwise and futile pursuit. If your peace and contentment are tied to something that comes and goes—and everything created comes and goes—then you are a hungry ghost chasing an empty illusion. Simply put, it's unwise to desire anything created.

> Misery doesn't arise because you don't have what you desire but because you desire what you don't have.

Desires lead to further desires without end because the momentary satisfaction of a desire will become unsatisfactory in the long run. It's guaranteed. The fulfillment of desires amounts to a hollow fulfillment—much like eating junk food that has lots of tasty flavor and calories but no nutritional value, shortly after which you feel hungry again. The real fulfillment is to realize that awareness is a state of boundless peace before the desire for something specific arises and creates an uncomfortable burning sensation to obtain it. The false self is the hungry ghost that tries to "trick" you into filling its insatiable cravings. Once you learn how the "trick" is done, the hungry ghost loses its ability to influence your behavior. Wisdom is the application of this knowledge and understanding. You are wise to the extent that you can sacrifice the immediate gratification of a desire, which is based on passing pleasure, for long-term peace, which is based on abiding contentment. *Your heart longs for abiding peace and contentment even though the body-mind has been conditioned to desire passing pleasure.*

If you look closely enough, you will discover that your heart's deepest wish is not to attain the object of desire time after time, which is a compulsive and highly uncomfortable state of agitation; your heart's deepest wish is to be free from the agitation of desire: simply to be at peace.

The Natural State

It's important that you come to see that you don't lack something inherently, that your natural state is one of rest, relaxation, and timeless peace. When you see desire as misguided and incapable of being fulfilled absolutely, you can begin to soften all desires back into formless presence, leaving awareness free of the superimposed agitation that created the illusion of lack where there was none.

Classic non-dual texts refer to the natural state as "being-consciousness-bliss," a compound description of *the simple contentment that you feel your self to be when you are free of the feeling of incompleteness*. The feeling of incompleteness was not original to you. The simple presence of awareness that I'm pointing to is pervaded by a sense of innate wellbeing that people almost always overlook in their fevered *desire* and *search* for wellbeing. When you stop identifying with desire and settle into your natural state of rest and relaxation, wellbeing glows with radiant warmth, and your natural abundance (or the abundance of nature) becomes increasingly self-evident.

You come to discover that you are naturally whole and complete and that you had simply been conditioned to think and feel otherwise. Awakening is not a "positive experience" or even a "gain" but simply the loss of the superimposed thought-feeling that there's something missing, lacking, or wrong. *There is nothing missing, lacking, or wrong!* There never was. Awakening leaves you as you *are*—before you began imagining lack in yourself and desiring objects to fill the imaginary void. As the presence of awareness, you're already fully present and aware and do not require any special efforts or attainments. What remains when desire for something "more" falls away is the fullness of needing nothing.

A disturbance in your timeless being only arises when you seek passing pleasure through some *particular* experience, which creates a painful sensation of self-contraction at the mental, emotional, and muscular levels. If you don't identify with the self-contractions and then soften them back into formlessness as soon as they arise, you begin to awaken to the natural state that never came or went by virtue of its timeless presence.

> The dismantling of the wanting-machine takes place every time you see it in operation without identifying with it.

You can think of dismantling the wanting-machine of desire as a devotional act of loving-kindness toward yourself. You can begin to do this once you have genuinely reached the limits of what you are able and willing to endure in terms of the suffering that results from wanting what you don't have or having what you don't want.

If you do not see this mechanism clearly, it will continue to recycle in a painful process of endless seeking. It drives profound loneliness and deep existential sadness. Many people turn to alcohol, drugs, and prescription medications, like antidepressants, to help them cope with these negative states. When you see clearly that it is precisely the programmed *seeking* of completion and happiness that is itself the felt sensation of lack and unhappiness, a great deal of your depression will subside and begin to heal naturally.

Being in nature can facilitate and even hasten this healing process. When you walk in a forest, for example, you immediately sense your kinship with nature. You feel your body-mind unwind and relax at a deep cellular level. Your ego and related desires melt away, and you are at peace. This process is exponentially more powerful when you allow yourself to *saunter*, a marvelous word that Henry David Thoreau uses to describe a sacred form of walking that does not have a destination in mind. Thoreau considers *sauntering* a lost art in the modern world and equates it with radical freedom insofar as it is predicated on leaving behind all your worldly concerns. As you saunter through nature, you resonate like a tuning fork with the peace and goodness of streams, bubbling brooks, wild animals, birds, moss, ferns, falling leaves, and trees, all of which are in the timeless natural state of what we would call "meditation." If you have ever watched a big animal at rest, you might have noticed how it's profoundly relaxed at a cellular level and breathes deeply. Big trees, such as redwoods and sequoias, similarly transmit a deeprooted presence with which the human body resonates on an ancient, primal, non-cognitive level. This can become your natural default state, too, when you allow yourself to fall back into the wideopen arms of boundless awareness instead of being in a constant unnatural state of fight, flight, or freeze. In fact, your body is already in the same natural state just like the rest of nature. Your body is already enlightened! It's just your *mind* that hasn't gotten the memo.

Desires vs. Preferences

In this context of the natural state, I would like to make a distinction between desires and preferences. It's an important one. Desires cause suffering because they indicate that your happiness is dependent upon a specific outcome; because they are dualistic and conditional, they are sticky and painful (you'll always "stick" to the side you want and feel the pain of that fixated adhesion). Simply put, if you suffer when you don't get what you want, you are in the painful grip of a desire.

When you begin to awaken, desire falls away, but you will probably still have *preferences*. Preferences indicate that you would *rather* one thing happen than another but that your peace will not be affected either way. Preferences are clean and natural. Therefore, they are healthier because you own your power by not allowing your state of being to fall prey to the mercy of circumstantial outcomes that are completely outside your control. Although desires may still arise after awakening, they won't cause suffering because they will have lost their "stickiness" by ceasing to revolve around or refer to a false self.

Awakening doesn't mean that you no longer experience pleasure and pain, only that your relationship to them changes radically. Prior to awakening, that is, the false self is in constant pursuit of pleasure and flight from pain. After awakening, pleasure and pain still arise, but instead of you going out of your self to pursue or reject them, they come to you. They are still experienced, in other words, but simply as the inevitable pleasures and pains of life. When you can enjoy whatever pleasure comes to you unsought and not reject whatever pain comes to you unsought, you are at peace.

To begin with, you can try simply to be content with what you already have and refuse to follow a desire for what you do not have. If that's not possible, sit with the seeking energy and soften into it until you are able to unhook your attention from it. Then you can begin to see that nothing created will completely satisfy your hunger because all created things are impermanent and empty of a reality apart from your true nature. Learning to rest as the formless natural state does require a process of maturation since most people's body-minds are addicted to desiring and seeking. Over time, though, you can recondition your system to be more in alignment with the peace of your true nature.

ON THE DESIRE FOR ROMANTIC RELATIONSHIPS

The desire for romantic relationships is perhaps the strongest desire and one of the stickiest areas for most people. When it comes to relationships, we as a species are culturally driven to find "the one." There are also biological reasons for this drive, as we humans are pack animals who for the most part crave companionship and relationship. Most people's single most persistent hope is to find a suitable mate; they think that if only they could find the right person, they would be happy. But it's not too difficult to see that this approach to happiness does not work. It's time to grow up! What if the relationship ends? In that case, they desperately search for a replacement and then find themselves in the same position when *that* relationship ends. And so it goes.

It's one of the most primal human instincts to seek relationship, connection, and intimacy, all of which are natural expressions of your true nature, but seeking them "outside" your self makes those qualities inaccessible by virtue of the separation you feel. The sensation of separation blocks the very thing the false self seeks in a vicious double bind.

Instead of trying to find someone ("the one") to fall in love with, fall in love with love ("the One"). In other words, fall in love with your true boundless self, for that boundless in-loveness contains all relative loves. As you drop down into the felt sense of being more and more, you will discover that your very own being radiates as boundless warmth and light without diminishing its infinite capacity to shine. When you relate primarily from that level and from the feeling that you yourself are the greatest love of your life despite all your shortcomings at the human level, you will *be* the unconditional love that you have been searching for.

Then, if a companion or relationship comes to you out of your fullness rather than out of desperation, you will be truly open to giving and receiving with genuine connection and intimacy instead of having a relationship that feverishly seeks those qualities on the quicksand of lack and neediness.

HOPELESSNESS IS YOUR ONLY HOPE

When you realize that you cannot maintain a permanent connection with anything created, including a romantic relationship, you come to a stunning conclusion: It's hopeless! In an ironic way, though, hopelessness signals the dawn of wisdom because it relieves you of the belief that you are in need of something better in the future. I don't mean "hopelessness" in the nihilistic sense, which can lead to an unhealthy feeling that life is pointless. If you can acknowledge through wisdom that hope for a better "future" is actually creating a sense of misery in the present, then you can finally begin to relax here and now and then root the body-mind into that wisdom. You can truly start to live and to enjoy the riches that already surround you rather than *hoping* to live a better life in a hypothetical future. Your system can begin to soften and rest as the underlying peace of your true self, which was the *relief* from desire and fear (i.e., the sense of peace) it was unwisely searching for in the imaginary realm of "the future." In that state of peace, life has tremendous color, vibrancy, aliveness, and beauty.

GUIDED MEDITATION: Shifting from Seeking Mode to Being Mode

To ensure that the pointers in this chapter do not remain at the level of intellectual understanding, let's take a moment to put into practice what we have been discussing so far. This meditation helps you shift from seeking mode to a relaxed state of being. To begin this meditation, choose a quiet space with limited distractions. You might even consider performing this meditation while taking a warm bath with sea salts for healing and candles for ambiance.

1. Sit or lie comfortably. Gently soften the thinking process and drop down into the felt sense of being, placing attention on the sensations of your body. If you notice any warmth or tingling, dwell on those sensations with your attention in order to get your attention out of the thinking process.

2. If you are still having a hard time softening the thinking process and dropping down into the felt sense of being, try focusing on the sensations of your in-and-out breath. Feel the cool air at the tip of your nose as you inhale or on the back of your throat as the air enters your lungs.

3. Soften any muscular tensions that are in your body, particu-
    larly those in your forehead, chest, and stomach—the three
    main focal points associated with mental, emotional, and
    primal seeking, respectively. Wish yourself well.

4. Notice if there is any seeking energy in your system. It could
    be for some food, the ending of this exercise, getting this
    meditation "right," and so forth.

5. If you detect any seeking energy, soften it as gently as pos-
    sible. Go slowly, microsecond by microsecond. Take your
    time to soften every movement of seeking back into the
    formless state.

6. As you track the sensations, can you notice that the seeking
    energy is flowing instead of solid? If the energy feels "stuck,"
    try thinking of it as a piece of ice that you are melting back
    into its formless state with a warm ray of loving awareness.

7. Can you notice that, right at this moment, you don't actu-
    ally *need* anything? If you are performing this meditation, it
    is highly likely that all your basic needs have been met. Rest
    your body-mind in the gratitude associated with having
    your basic needs met.

8. Again notice if there are any thoughts arising that are
    dwelling on the past or seeking fulfillment in the future. It
    could be an old painful memory or a desire for a snack.
    Simply notice the thought and gently withdraw the projec-
    tion of that fantasy, relaxing back into your felt sense of
    being.

9. Dwell in this rested state for some time, at least three to five
    minutes, before gently reintegrating back into your daily
    rhythm. Don't rush into activity.

10. Reflect on what you have discovered in this meditation, perhaps over a soothing cup of herbal tea.

Ideally you will have noticed in this guided meditation how all desires and muscular tensions are dreamt up with insubstantial, fleeting thoughts and sensations. Hopefully you could sense the energetic deliciousness of rest and relaxation when you are not being *unnaturally* self-contracted. Seeking is just the energetic signature of a body-mind that is confused about what it's looking for. The more you switch from seeking mode to being mode, the more you will feel simply content.

Noticing the Gap Between Your Thoughts

The previous guided meditation focused specifically on softening compulsive thinking and muscular tensions, inviting you to rest in the felt sense of being. This is an extremely important thing to learn since most people's desiring and seeking begins either at the level of compulsive thinking or at the level of bodily sensations where certain subtle muscular contractions drive the system into a state of agitation and even frenzy.

I'd like now to suggest the importance of not just softening the thinking process, but noticing the soft gap *between* thoughts. Since most people's thinking has an obsessive quality that often propels their system into endless frantic activity, it's extremely helpful to awaken to the fact that thoughts have restful gaps between them. Many people don't even know that they are capable of watching their thoughts, let alone becoming aware of the gap between them.

> The fact that you can watch your thoughts, sensations, and emotions serves as the entry point to and the token of freedom.

This capacity of metacognition, of watching your inner state instead of being completely identified with it, is what separates you from other life forms that are wholly identified with (and bound to) the pleasure-pain nexus. It's also why the ancient non-dual texts consider a human birth exceptionally auspicious. Once you know that you have the ability not to identify with thoughts, sensations, and emotions and to rest in the gap between them, you as consciousness actually have a choice about whether or not you suffer. Then, and only then, do you as the living, sentient principle of life have a real choice. Prior to that realization, your thoughts, sensations, and emotions will unconsciously drive your behavior out of the momentum of conditioning or the magnetism of habit-patterns.

It's so hard to perceive this gap at first because thoughts are not only in tension through many years of running on autopilot, but they are in an almost constant state of convulsion that creates a subtle yet powerful sensation of self-contraction with which most people remain perpetually identified without knowing it. This is also why the state of personal identification may be called a state of "ignorance," a literal *not knowing* that invites compassion instead of criticism from those who do know toward those who don't. When you begin to soften the compulsive thinking process, to watch thoughts dispassionately, and to rest in the gap between them, you may experience a mental charley horse. Headaches are common in the early stages. Most people are so habituated to focusing on one specific thought after another that the attention recoils when it's invited to dwell peacefully between two specific thoughts. Thoughts have a "grabby" and "sticky" quality or, as I will discuss in the next chapter, a hypnotic pull. But the really good news is that this hypnotic pull can be weakened or dispelled over time with practice.

GUIDED MEDITATION: Resting in the Gap Between Your Thoughts

The more you soften the mental grip over and over again, giving yourself permission simply to be at peace, the more the natural state of peaceful rest and relaxation becomes self-evident to you. At first, you may have to do this repeatedly since your thoughts will continue knotting up. Eventually it becomes effortless. The purpose of this guided meditation is to realize that *your mental state is in a natural condition of empty, peaceful relaxation between your thoughts.* You will come to see that this natural state of empty, peaceful relaxation just becomes obscured by a convulsive process of thinking and of related muscular tension that sucks all your attention by sheer force of habit. To continue this process of relaxing back into your natural state, I invite you to try the following meditation first thing in the morning— before you have had coffee, tea, or any other kind of stimulant (including visual stimulants such as your smartphone or TV). Caffeine is particularly notorious for stimulating thought-activity and makes this process more challenging than it needs to be. When you first wake up in the morning, your attention is still soft and open.

1. Sit or lie comfortably. It's important not to place any pressure on the body or mind.

2. Using the techniques of relaxation that you learned in the last guided meditation, soften any muscular tensions in the body. Soften the thinking process, too.

3. Become aware of the flow of thoughts. Do this for two to three minutes.

4. Now, instead of focusing on the *flow* of thoughts, watch each thought arise and subside like waves on an ocean. Do this for two to three minutes.

5. Now try to soften your thought activity even more, relaxing the brain as though it were a muscle, and become aware of the soft, subtle gap *between* your thoughts. That gap is peace itself.

6. Imagine the gap between your thoughts as the sweet nectar inside a flower. Use your attention like the long, thin beak of a hummingbird to extract the nectar. Sip on the delicious nectar for one or two seconds at a time, nourishing yourself on its sweetness with each brief sip.

7. Now, drop the image of the hummingbird and try for three to five seconds at a time to sustain unbroken awareness of the soft, sweet, silent gap between your thoughts. During those times of unbroken awareness, notice how good you feel. Rest in that goodness.

8. If this is challenging for you and you become frustrated at any point, allow your frustration to arise, softening your resistance to it and any self-judgment you might have. Have compassion for yourself; this is a new way of being that takes practice. Then try the exercises again in a softened, relaxed state of open receptivity.

9. What was your experience? Did you feel free of mental agitation or at least less mentally agitated during these times?

10. Reflect on this exercise for two to three minutes before continuing to read.

By watching your stream of thinking objectively, becoming aware of the gap between your thoughts, and resting in that gap, your awakening is well underway. Performing this guided meditation officially signals the dawn of wisdom and, if you stick with it, can replace your seeking mind with a peaceful one. The gap between thoughts has a tremendous amount of power, so much so that simply resting in the gap for a few seconds at a time produces a radiation of joy and releases a huge amount of relief, gratitude, and love.

As I suggested above, you can taste this complete relaxation quite easily when you first wake up in the morning; for at least a few seconds before thinking kicks in, you are conscious and totally at peace. You might try to notice this window of conscious peace when you first wake up in the morning and then try to rest in it for as long as possible, at least twenty minutes. This tiny window, which can grow the more you prolong it, is convincing proof that peace is actually your true nature. You simply might never have *noticed* it.

The Importance of Self-Care

The main point of this chapter was to highlight the importance of taking care of yourself and wishing yourself well as a default mode. The guided meditations in this chapter are essentially forms of self-care. As you have probably noticed, our culture in general often makes self-care difficult. This is particularly true when it comes to the news, which is fear-driven and characterized by an increasingly toxic spectacle that verges on and even lapses into the burlesque. In fact, the news has become a form of "infotainment," a postmodern pastiche of information and ratings-driven entertainment that generates and perpetuates negative states, often making it difficult for people to feel well or to see things as they are.

I would suggest that the modern media, especially the news media, should be approached with extreme caution. At the very least, you might consider limiting the amount of news that you watch or read, especially as you are just beginning to awaken. The repetition of sound bites, coupled with a potent mix of disturbing words and images, has a deeply traumatic effect on the body-mind. By plugging into mainstream news, especially if you're a "news junkie," you will likely see the world from within the dis-eased perspective of "the consensus reality," which activates and agitates the nervous system. Simply put, the news often functions as a distorted filter that makes life appear a certain way—mostly existentially dreadful. When people feel that way, they consume more products in the vain hopes that those temporary things will make them feel better, take more prescription drugs, like antidepressants and medications for things like high blood pressure, and drink more alcohol to numb out altogether. I can assure you that it is not in the best interests of corporations for people to feel well. As that scene from *Annie Hall* suggests, people are so invisibly used to feeling miserable that they just think that's life or that's the human condition. But the point I'm making is that it doesn't have to be! There are actually many wonderful things happening in the world that you would never know about if you only watched the mainstream news.

Rather than feeling awful about things over which you have no control, you might consider the possibility of taking control over what you consume with your senses. As a general rule, I would suggest that you stop taking in or doing anything that disturbs your wellbeing. I don't want to be prescriptive, and I'm not suggesting that you stick your head in the sand or that you become a recluse; I'm simply inviting you to take stock of your patterns of consumption that may be causing you unnecessary suffering and then, with your best interests at heart, to release them because they do not serve you. You actually have the power to create and shape your own destiny rather than having it imposed on you by your culture. It's important to discover as a first step that you are in charge of the world in which you live. Despite how it appears, the *way* you experience life is not imposed upon you. Generally speaking, each human being lives in a private bubble-world of his or her own making. You only ever live in a limited world dominated by desire and fear because you subconsciously consent to it. The bare events are the universal aspect of experience; the *interpretation* of those events constitutes the private, limited aspect that takes place in the virtual reality of memory and imagination, which is where most human beings live and die.

Relatively speaking, reality consists of whatever happens minus your thoughts.

Instead of fighting against or within a distorted world that does not exist the way you *think* it does, the best way forward is to unplug from the consensus reality, to wake up to your true nature, and to start embodying a more authentic life that's not shaped by the dominant dis-eased culture. Otherwise you merely feed the illness and give it life with your interest and attention. I invite you to tune in only to those books, movies, TV shows, songs, and Internet sites that truly inspire you to fulfill your greatest potential for evolution and self-knowledge. When you shift to those uplifting frequencies and let go of those that contract your sense of wellbeing, your life (and the lives around you) will automatically begin to heal.

I'm suggesting that taking the best possible care of yourself is not only the best thing you can do for *yourself* but also for the *world*. There may be rare instances where you are compelled to sacrifice your own wellbeing—for example, if you leap to someone's aid at the potential expense of your own safety or if you are living in a traumatic environment, such as a war-torn country where you are in survival mode. But if you *routinely* put others before yourself at the expense of your own wellbeing or do things that subconsciously traumatize your psyche despite the fact that they're "normalized" (such as watching violent movies and TV shows), you are actually doing yourself harm. The true meaning of "self-love" is to put what is truly good for you first: that is, to do everything in your power *to wake up* to your innate radiance, wholeness, and perfection. It is a beautiful gesture of honoring the sanctity of your own life and potential.

Once you have a healthy perspective with a grounded insight into your true nature, you are free to serve the world with wisdom as the foundation. Otherwise, you may aggravate the situation and make it worse, adding to suffering rather than alleviating it.

Awakening, therefore, is not "selfish"; it is an invaluable gift to humanity, partly because you will no longer be adding *more* suffering to the situation. Furthermore, because you are not separate from the whole, shaping your own destiny in the light of your evolutionary awakening will automatically impact the destiny of the entire species and even the planet. You awaken, in other words, both for yourself and for the benefit of the totality.

A Quick Review

This chapter explained and experientially demonstrated how the desire and search for something "more" causes misery and obscures the natural state of peaceful contentment that abides here and now. By softening your compulsive thinking process and muscular tensions, you can begin to rest in the benevolent substratum of your true nature instead of creating and perpetuating the conditions for your own ill-being. I ended this chapter with a suggestion to take the best possible care of yourself as a devotional act of self-love. As you stop doing things that are harmful or toxic to your innate sense of wellbeing, you will not only feel less miserable, but your energetic countenance will glow and you will be motivated to awaken fully into your boundless potential. We also discussed how your evolution toward greater self-knowledge positively impacts the collective because you are not separate from the whole of life.

In the next chapter, I discuss how the prevailing worldview of scientific materialism, which discounts or dismisses awareness, does a lot of harm both to humans and to our environment. By pointing out how people become deadened to their experience and then providing a more holistic, animated worldview based on the centrality of radiant awareness, I shed further light not only on the peace and contentment that abide here and now, but also on the spiritual brilliance of your true nature.

CHAPTER 2

AN ALTERNATIVE WORLDVIEW

Although it works undeniably well on a surface level of experience and has made some remarkably positive advancements, conventional Western science largely functions by way of a materialistic paradigm that does a lot of harm both to human beings and to our habitats. It also largely ignores consciousness, considering it "unscientific." Conventional science will never solve what David Chalmers famously called "the hard problem of consciousness" until it comes to the conclusion that consciousness serves as the primary, unifying, fundamental ground of experience rather than being the incidental "epiphenomenon" of material processes that are mechanical and meaningless in nature.

That is, the conventional Western scientific worldview projects a materialistic, artificially mechanistic structure onto the integral nature of the living reality. For example, mainstream scientists often compare the body to a machine, reduce life to a computerized flow of "information," view matter as inanimate, conceptualize DNA as the "building blocks" of life, and suggest that the sequencing of genes can tell us something about life itself. Conventional Western science pulls things apart to study them and, generally speaking, does not take into account holistic interdependence. By unnaturally separating the seamless fabric of life into discrete conceptual categories without putting them back together again, scientific materialism unwittingly projects a dream of "the world" as a collection of separate, independently existing material components rather than honoring the fact that everything we experience is part of a single integrated, living system. Life is not computerized and mechanistic, full of random "bits of information"; it is conscious, non-conceptually intelligent, and altogether miraculous. If you think about it, whatever is happening at conception with the sperm and egg is not a material process. It is conscious spirit meeting conscious spirit.

As we project a collective dream of "the world" based on the limitations of the scientific paradigm, we project a similar worldview at the individual level with the dream of "my life." We forget that we made up all the divisions, classifications, and labels and that reality does not share the limited ideas we have about it. We convert the inexplicable reality into graspable concepts and subsist within a linear framework instead of living in tune with the fact that, although causation works relatively well for conventional purposes, organic spontaneity characterizes life itself. The term "predictable life" is an oxymoron. If your life is completely predictable, it almost certainly lacks vitality.

The false assumptions that form the basis of scientific materialism and of human culture in general are at the root of the misery that we examined in the last chapter. When you have a material worldview, you will be materialistic to some degree; you will want more and more stuff to fill the void you feel as a consequence of the materialistic worldview you have! The false assumptions of the materialistic worldview are also responsible for our systematic destruction of the planetary ecosystem with which all of us are braided. When you view the world as "lifeless" and "other," you can kick it around and exploit it. We do that not only with each other, but also with the environment. The unnatural split between humans and the environment turns out to be a position of literal insanity; it's inherently violent, exploitative, and manipulative. Instead of cooperating with the environment that sustains us, we apply a militaristic attitude that somehow rationalizes a drive to "divide and conquer" it. Even when it comes to natural diseases or even death, we wage "battles" and "wars" against them and try to overpower them through sheer force of will. We can no longer afford to live in alienation and fear, nor can we afford to have anything less than a conscious, spirit-based perspective that values the sanctity of all things. We and the Earth have suffered enough; it's time to wake up.

Our exploitation and manipulation of the environment certainly has certain benefits on the conventional level. We have made huge strides in technology and medical treatment, for example. But the costs of scientific materialism are profound and clearly outweigh the benefits if we do not balance technological advancement with more holistic modalities of integrative health, with humanistic values, and with a sacred view of life. We live longer lives but at the cost of our sanity and wellbeing. We in "developed" nations have abundant resources but at the cost of rain forests, entire species, ocean health, the ozone layer, and the contentment and joy that come with the simple fulfillment of basic needs. It's not a good deal—certainly not a wise one. Unless we balance technological evolution with an evolution of consciousness, the imbalance will destroy us and possibly all life on Earth.

The purpose of this chapter is to provide you with an overview of an alternative worldview that places awareness or consciousness at the center of experience and establishes the importance of having a holistic, animated view of life. I hope to displace the false worldview based on scientific materialism, analyze the trauma associated with the conventional model of life, and draw your attention experientially to the radiant aliveness of awareness. Ideally this chapter will awaken you to the preciousness of your true nature, enable you to notice and appreciate the spiritual brilliance of awareness, and inspire you to delve more deeply into your true nature in subsequent chapters.

The Basic Mistakes

For all the complexity of the human experience, the false worldview hinges on several simple, innocent mistakes that result in all the chaos we see in our lives and in the news on a daily basis. These mistakes are based on unnatural divisions, separations, and limitations, all of which we'll be examining and deconstructing throughout this book. Basically, the consensus reality rests on the following mistaken interpretations of experience:

1. The universe (including space and time) is an objective, independently existing phenomenon.

2. The objects of experience are made of inanimate matter.

3. You are a separate self.

4. There is a division between "inner" and "outer" experience.

5. Awareness is located and contained "inside" your head.

The exact opposite interpretations are closer to the truth. However, the misinterpretations of experience have become so normalized that it's extremely difficult to see the errors in the mistaken worldview once they harden as cognitive structures of experience.

The reason for this is that we humans have a bewitching capacity to conceptualize and to imagine, and without realizing it, we become absorbed in our *ideas* about reality rather than inhabiting the vibrancy of conscious experience as we did in childhood. We create virtual problems and then try desperately to solve them on their own level. Because all concepts are removed from reality, they act as cataracts that obscure direct experience—or act as calluses that deaden the vibrant sensitivity of sensation and perception. Because they are familiar, we hang onto our concepts for dear life, as they supply a false sense of security against the void that constantly threatens the false self with extinction.

The effects of these mistakes are profound. They make people feel painfully separate and limited. When you see and feel the consequences of this way of being, it is clear that the consensus reality just doesn't work at the mental, emotional, and somatic levels. It just plain *hurts*. We are in need of a more sacred, holistic view of life.

A New Model of Life

As an alternative to the worldview based on the consensus reality, this book presents a new yet ancient worldview for your consideration that's based on the primacy of creative awareness. The purpose of this new way of experiencing is to wake you up from the sleep of fearful separation and to restore your original shine as radiant, boundless awareness.

When you conceptually divide the indivisible ground of experience into discreet mental categories and believe that these categories refer to things that exist independently of conscious experience, life becomes dull, repetitive, meaningless, and random. As you will come to see directly in your progressive journey through this book, you do not passively see, feel, taste, touch, and smell. Awareness, as the creative principle of life, is actively experiencing itself in the subjective forms of the senses. The senses are *forms of subjective knowledge*. But what exactly *is* subjective knowledge? Pure magic.

Because quantum physics is so paradoxical, it has done a lot to facilitate a shift in worldview from the mechanical to the magical and has even led to some fascinating connections between science and spirituality. But the mainstream Western scientific establishment continues to work largely within the paradigm that we can perceive and study the world "objectively"—in other words, that we are apart or separate from nature—and that consciousness has no real place in scientific endeavor since it can't be "proven" objectively.

However, we are not separate from the totality of nature—the body, after all, *is* nature—and before any scientific experiment or any experience can begin, consciousness must be present. To appropriate Wallace Stevens's wonderful book title, it's "the necessary angel." It cannot be dismissed or even discounted to secondary importance because it's the very basis for the arising of all knowledge and experience. In fact, consciousness and experience cannot be pulled apart because the observer and the observed are indivisible; *they are two ways of conceptually labeling a single experience.* The "observer effect" in quantum physics substantiates this claim by demonstrating scientifically that the act of observing influences the phenomenon being observed. As J. Krishnamurti used to say, "The observer *is* the observed." Although modern conventional science considers the observer effect an embarrassment because it does not fit into its materialistic paradigm, it should be a huge clue about the importance and even the centrality of consciousness to experience.

It's true that consciousness (i.e., the "observer") has no material or objective qualities, but it's important to reiterate the fact that it cannot be discounted or ignored. Interestingly, when you look for the conscious factor that is lighting up the show, it cannot be grasped or even *found* as such. To adapt a paradoxical phrase from the Christian mystical tradition, consciousness is an "uncreated light."

Consciousness is also breathtakingly intelligent and efficient; it's growing trees, weaving the tissues of your body together, beating your heart, and spontaneously animating countless physiological processes without lifting a finger. It is the ultimate meaning of beauty, truth, and goodness.

The first step to waking up is to become conscious that there is consciousness. This simple shift produces a staggering, awe-inspiring realization that somehow eludes our attention and appreciation: *there is consciousness.* How? Why? There's no answer to these questions. No one can say. All we know for sure is that consciousness *is*. It's an inexplicable fact. To use the Zen phrase, it's "empty and marvelous." Consciousness is the greatest mystery shining in full evidence.

But I prefer to think of this work as an inquiry into the nature of reality. In fact, we are being "realists" in the highest, most literal sense of that word. It's just that upon close examination, the source and substance of experience turns out to be what we call "spirit" since it has no material qualities. It's beyond the senses (and therefore "transcendental") but even *more* certain than sensory perceptions because the senses function by virtue of the presence of consciousness. It doesn't have to be "achieved" because it's already present. It's just extremely *subtle* and can only be known intuitively.

> We can think of consciousness or awareness in terms of subtlety but not in terms of distance or achievement.

This simple realization merely requires an intuitive "pointing out" and an equally intuitive insight to confirm its presence, its hereness. It is *so* self-evident that it goes without saying!

Robots Are Not Sentient

Let's take a moment to ponder conscious light—to consider the significance that there is consciousness. First, consider a video camera and a robot. Both are computerized devices that have the capacity to process information and to produce bare facsimiles of experience. A video camera, for example, can record visual scenes, and a robot can scan its environment for objects and navigate around them relatively well. However, what these devices do *not* possess is the capacity to have a *subjective experience*, the sense of consciousness, awareness, or sentience that characterizes life itself. A robot can be programmed to speak the words "I exist," but it would not be able to understand the significance of that statement. Neither a video camera nor a robot can *know* or *experience* anything. They lack *sentience*. Your smartphone is "smart" in the sense that it can be programmed with tons of information, but it is not intelligent. It cannot appreciate the smell of coffee, the beauty of a symphony by Beethoven, or the feeling of love. All that takes *intelligence*. There is a difference not just in degree but in *kind* between "artificial intelligence" and the intelligence of life itself; despite our science fiction fantasies, never the twain shall meet.

Just as the world appears lifelessly within the insentient lens of the camera, the world appears *full of life* within the sentient, intelligent, animating lens of your subjectivity. Whatever you experience *is* your subjectivity. It's illuminated by conscious light or what my early teacher Toni Packer called "awaring"—otherwise you would not have any knowledge of the experience, which would be tantamount to the experience not existing or merely existing in a potential state. Your subjectivity evokes the world of experience out of the potential state into a state of (momentary) actuality.

GUIDED MEDITATION: Being Aware of Being Aware

In your experience right now, there is consciousness, but you may have become desensitized to this wondrous fact. In this guided meditation, you won't become conscious, for consciousness is already present. Instead, you will become *conscious* that there is consciousness—what Nisargadatta Maharaj calls "aware of being aware." This meditation ideally calls for a video camera or a digital photo camera as a prop, but even if you don't have one, you can still do the exercise.

1. Take a few moments to relax any tensions in your body. Take a few deep breaths.

2. If you have a video camera or a digital picture camera, perhaps on your smartphone, turn it on. (If you don't have one, you can just imagine this scenario.)

3. You don't have to record anything; just look at the moving image in the screen on your device as you pan the environment. Is your camera aware of the scene? Is it "seeing" anything? How does the camera feel from its own perspective? Does it feel *anything*?

4. Now put the camera down and scan the environment not like a video camera but as your conscious self. Become aware of being aware. What does *that* feel like?

5. Now contemplate the difference between the way *you* see and the way a camera sees. *Feel into and be that difference.* What does it feel like? (You can use any one of the five senses for this meditation.)

6. Remain in the wonderment of this contemplation for at least three to five minutes, also allowing the body to vibrate with the felt, kinesthetic implications of any experiential insights that may have been triggered.

Hopefully this guided meditation made you aware of being aware and kindled wonder regarding the extraordinary presence of awareness. This book is largely an investigation into—and celebration of—the difference that you have discovered in this meditation. Whatever it is, that difference is the most vital aspect of life since *it evokes experience and knowledge*. It is your greatest treasure and is what separates you from an automaton. When you ignore or are asleep to your self as conscious light, you are *like* an automaton that just scans the world passively or robotically, dead to the aliveness that you are.

It's helpful at first to perform this meditation repeatedly. Keep noticing how miraculous it is that *there is the sense of subjective experience*, not just a robotic, inert scanning or recording of a lifeless physical environment. Being aware of being aware is a sort of juicy, vibrant knowing. Throughout your day, even for short moments at a time, keep sensing and feeling into this perspective intuitively, as though you were immersing your experience in a bath of warm water. Allow your entire being to fall in love with and to become ravished by this contemplation, soaking in that love and ravishment for as long as possible. You will find that, far from being a cold and lifeless nothingness or "void," conscious light is almost unbearably sweet and precious. It is full of heart. The more you soak in the state of *being aware of being aware* like fruit in a mixture of honey and brandy, the more it dawns on you that you are benevolent wellbeing itself, pouring your intoxicating sweetness on whatever you gaze upon.

The Radiance of an Old Pair of Shoes

Vincent van Gogh's still life oil painting from 1886 entitled *A Pair of Shoes* beautifully illustrates the aliveness of awareness and in many ways expresses the main theme of this book. I would recommend that you take a moment to look the painting up online in order to follow along with my description and interpretation.*

The painting can be interpreted in countless ways, and in fact, this particular painting has been the subject of philosophical debate for many years. It depicts an old pair of worn-out shoes that van Gogh bought at a Paris flea market.

For me, the beauty of the painting lies in the juxtaposition of the ordinariness of a seemingly material "thing" that could not be more inconsequential from a conventional perspective with the stunningly illuminated background against which the shoes stand out and in which the shoes themselves participate. The radiance of the bright gold background, which the shoes reflect with glimmers of gold on the tattered leather and laces, produces a sort of halo effect that divinizes and brings to life the most mundane of objects, something that most of us would never stop to *see* let alone appreciate. Most of

---

* A very good reproduction can be found on Wikimedia Commons: https://commons.wikimedia.org/wiki/File:Van_Gogh_-_Ein_Paar_Schuhe.jpeg.

us go through life *looking* at everything but not *seeing* anything. Looking is passive and inanimate; seeing is aliveness itself. Like all great artists, van Gogh transmutes looking into seeing, waking awareness up to the vibrancy of conscious being. The gold in the oval circumference at the center of the painting is *so* bright and luminescent that it subtly fades into and verges on pure white light. The shoes are radiant in their simple *is*-ness. *They are alive.* Isn't it miraculous that a pair of shoes exists rather than not? Is the existence of a pair of old shoes any less likely or amazing than the existence of *anything*? That *anything* appears should be cause for awe and wonder. The ordinary *is* extra-ordinary; the natural *is* super-natural.

In our context, I suggest that the painting wakes awareness up to the fact that it shines radiantly as the entire field of experience. It draws attention to the glorious beauty of conscious light—suggesting that true beauty is not ultimately in *what* you perceive but in the fact *that* you perceive. Seemingly ordinary material objects just sit there in their *is*-ness, waiting and almost begging to be seen as they are: ablaze with creative, loving awareness.

A New Way of Seeing and Being

There's a wonderful quotation by the great French novelist Marcel Proust: "My destination is no longer a place but, rather, a new way of seeing." As you go through your day, put this "new way of seeing" (and being) into practice. Whenever it occurs to you, try seeing and feeling *as* this vivid, alive, spiritual, mysterious subjective awareness. Try it not only when you look at the environment, but also, and even especially, when you look at other people. Because interpersonal exchanges often trigger deep precognitive fears that can result in minor to acute forms of self-contraction, you will initially need to remain steady (i.e., awake) by consciously softening whatever tensions may arise, especially those in the solar plexus and head. The muscles around the eyes are notoriously connected to these self-contractions. Practicing this shift even for a few moments at a time has a powerful transformative and healing effect on the body-mind and on the entire field of experiencing. Over time, the need for "practice" drops away once this sacred way of perceiving becomes established as the natural state.

A Quick Review

In this chapter, I drew a sharp distinction between the conventional worldview based on scientific materialism and a model of life based on the primacy of awareness. Rather than living within a mechanistic paradigm, I invited you to notice and appreciate the spiritual brilliance and significance of sentience. Hopefully the guided meditation kindled awe and wonder in you and triggered you to become aware of being aware. In the next chapter, we'll examine how your sense of being a separate, contained self was literally installed by hypnotic suggestion from infancy onward. By understanding this process of ego development and heeding a call from your heart to evolve into deeper regions of truth, you can begin to come out of the egoic state of consciousness by a process of self-emptying. As you remain earnestly committed to this natural evolutionary unfoldment, you will very quickly start to live as the boundless love and light that you truly are.

CHAPTER 3

THE TRANCE OF MISIDENTIFICATION

When I was young, I saw a performer who made a lasting impression on me. He was a hypnotist, and he would call various people up from the audience and hypnotize them into believing they were someone or something else. The one that truly amazed me was when he hypnotized a woman into believing that she was a chicken; she started running around the stage like a chicken, clucking and everything! I marveled at this phenomenon and wondered how on earth that was possible.

Many years later, I saw an interview with a hypnotist who did the same thing. He said something interesting that now makes perfect sense to me. Before the performance, he would stand outside the hall watching the audience members file into the auditorium, taking particular note of those people who looked especially suggestible—those who had a "vacant," "dull," or "dopey" look in their eyes, for instance. When the performance began, he would pick out those people to hypnotize, the gullible-looking ones he had previously selected. Basically, he was using his keen powers of observation in the realm of human psychology and applying his knowledge of people's susceptibility to subliminal programming.

What I came to see was that when people believed what others told them, the thoughts in their head, and the stories that revolve around their egoic sense of self, awareness is being hypnotized in the same way that the hypnotist was hypnotizing his participants. When people believe their thoughts about anything other than purely functional matters, it's usually not pretty! They essentially start to run around and cluck like a chicken. The separate psychologically driven, thought-based identity is as false as the chicken identity. They are both superimposed onto the true formless nature of awareness, which has the capacity and the tendency to become hypnotized by its own mesmerizing expressions. The movement of thoughts (and emotions) has a soporific quality just like a pocket watch that a hypnotist swings back and forth; it puts awareness to sleep and creates a dream of personal identity.

This is a completely innocent process because awareness is fundamentally innocent; in its innocence, it eagerly identifies with every thought and emotion that arises. It's exquisitely sensitive and responsive. Awareness doesn't know any better until it finally wakes up to its true nature through the wisdom of experiential insight. No one could be blamed or criticized for being subliminally programmed, as he or she is by definition not in control of that process. In that sense, too, everyone is "innocent," though someone's behavior might well be unacceptable and might still have practical consequences. The realization of everyone's essential innocence does not *excuse* unskillful or harmful behavior; it simply explains it. This realization also allows us to develop compassion rather than hatred in our hearts for those who are unconsciously identified with their negative conditioning.

A spiritual teacher is someone who calls to your attention that you are hypnotized by limiting beliefs and then de-hypnotizes you by bringing you out of the state of hypnotic identification with trance-inducing thoughts and emotions—essentially reminding you that you're not a "chicken." Once you are aware that you are programmed with limiting beliefs, you have more of a choice about your behavior. You can then begin to empty yourself of those limiting patterns, which allows true freedom to emerge. Waking up is not about adding something onto awareness; it's about subtracting the identification with false limiting beliefs that create wacky behavior on the stage of this variety show called "life." It's about coming out of a hypnotic state.

Before you can awaken to this truth fully and stop clucking like a chicken, as it were, it is first helpful to understand how awareness initially became entranced by thoughts and how you appear to have become a separate self, resulting in the illusion of limitation and all the feverish seeking that results. This chapter describes how the mesmerism of the separate self comes about from infancy onward and how it is based on subliminal programming.

How the Separate Self Forms

When you were born, your sense of self had not formed yet. You had no defenses, no armor, no self to protect. You were just pure conscious love and light. If you look into a baby's eyes, you will be reminded of your own innocence and the unconditional love that you came into the world with. While looking into a baby's eyes, your heart will instantly melt into a puddle because the baby is devoid of psychological identity and of all the ego, judgment, opinion, and hatred that come with conditioning. You will see the adorable nature of awareness in its pure and innocent state. People love their pets for the same reason.

Slowly, the baby starts to learn a language, to become conditioned, to develop a sense of self, to become willful, to become self-protected, and to acquire one limiting belief after another. Essentially the child comes to feel essentially wounded and in need of being healed of a sense of separation from his or her original wholeness. But those conditioned layers of self-identity are entirely conceptual and relative to a more authentic self that is not itself in need of being healed. You are capable of discovering that authentic self through the process of awakening to your original nature. Awakening entails a beautiful evolutionary process of love unfolding to its deepest potential. Your heart yearns for this discovery. Awakening is the only thing that will ultimately "heal" you—not because there's something inherently wrong with you but because you have come to believe there is.

> Awakening heals you of the belief that you need to be healed.

Despite what you may think or feel, you never actually lose the innocence, unconditional love, and adorable quality of pure awareness that you were born with. You just come to *believe* you did through a process of auto-suggestion. Paradoxically, your innocence is restored when you realize that it was never tarnished.

The Mesmerism of the I-Thought

The belief that awareness is separate, limited, contained, and private rests on a spectacular illusion created by what Ramana Maharshi calls the "I-thought." He uses that phrase to distinguish it from the true "I" of formless, universal awareness. The I-thought refers to an acquired conceptual identity, your belief that "I am so-and-so" based on what others told you. The "I" started to form somewhere between the age of three and five years old when you began to think of yourself as a separate, contained self with personal agency. It's called the "I-thought" because it's a recurring thought made of the pronoun "I" that creates the mirage of separate agency. The sense is that "I" am doing this or that, rather than just having the sense that this or that is happening spontaneously. The I-thought creates a mirage of separate willfulness. To use a simile, this mirage appears much like the mirage of an oasis in a desert. When the sun shines intensely on the desert sand, it creates a shimmer that appears from a distance as water, but of course there's no water there. You could never walk up to it, touch it, or drink it. It's a mirage. Similarly, when awareness shines intensely on the desert sand of the mind, so to speak, it creates a shimmering "I-thought" that appears to you as a separate doer, but there's no "I" there. You could never locate or grasp it. It's a conceptual mirage.

This process of becoming entranced by the mirage of the I-thought crept up on you well before you were aware that it was happening. As an infant and young child, you were literally in a hypnogogic state where you subliminally soaked up *everything* that was said and felt around you—not only from family members and teachers, but also from all the movies, TV shows, radio programs, news, and commercials that were running in the background wherever you went. Your "programs" (that is, your limiting subconscious belief systems) were "installed" in this early period, and since your family members most likely weren't awakened, you inherited their programs, too. Generational programs are good old-fashioned heirlooms.

Many of your deepest programs were shaped in relation to the primal wounds associated not only with birth, but also with existentially uncomfortable experiences related to pain, hunger, trauma, and unmet needs. These primal wounds were deeply embedded in cell memory because they shocked the soft innocence of your system, which contracted in the presence of discomfort like an amoeba toward a toxin. Repeated patterns of self-contraction based on fear and desire slowly led to a tendency in boundless awareness to contract out of self-protection as a way of life. These contractions happened subconsciously at the mental, emotional, and muscular levels and were powerfully correlated with the physical image of your body reflected in the mirror. The contractions were also strengthened in infancy through verbal cues (by people continuously pointing to your body and telling you to say your name, for instance). By identifying with your body and mind, you started to feel like an object.

When you first began to internalize the sense of objectification, you started to believe deep down in your being that "I am inside this body." The feeling was "I am so-and-so." You also started to acquire all the limiting beliefs based on the I-thought: "I am unlovable," "I am stupid," "I am a klutz," "I am not attractive," "I am broken," "I am wounded," and so forth. The I-thought, which is actually an *object* of perception, began to take the place of your true limitless subjectivity and to eclipse the conscious love and light that you truly were—the conscious love and light you never stop being, which is the same conscious love and light that shines in everyone's eyes as a little gleam of light.

> The I-thought created the illusion of containment when you came to associate it with awareness.

As the I-thought formed, everything simultaneously was put at odds with your separate sense of self. The belief that the world was "outside" you arose in relation to the separate self "inside" you. The separate "I" and the separate "other" depend on each other and are in fact co-created.

Over time, therefore, your formless being and boundless heart came to associate exclusively with a psychosomatic impression of yourself as a minuscule object at odds with a much bigger collection of objects that make up "the world." It resulted in feeling like "I am the tiny nucleus of a bewildering cacophony of experience." But you are now waking up to the fact that this nucleus is nothing more than a combination of a conceptual sense of yourself and a painful conglomeration of dense, self-contracted muscular tensions in the body.

Your sense of containment was also strengthened by shocking verbal cues. When you were being a rambunctious little boy or girl, for example, your parents might have scolded you by saying, "Contain yourself!" This kind of verbal instruction makes a deep, lasting impression on memory, forcing your innocence to self-contract out of fear and to feel painfully self-conscious about your behavior. You started to feel like a creaturely object that was doing something wrong.

Since all objects are limited, feeling like an object produces a lifelong sense that something is missing; it is this nagging feeling that compels you to attempt to fill that void with other objects like material possessions—an altogether hopeless task, as we have seen, since that feeling of limitation cannot ever be permanently assuaged on its own level. It feels like a state of worthlessness, of never feeling good or full enough. You have to come out of that state altogether by seeing clearly how your identification with the false psychosomatic self is the primary source of all your beliefs and feelings of lack, limitation, and neediness.

You must also see how you are no longer in need of self-protection because your true self is not actually vulnerable. It is innocent, but it is not vulnerable. Your self-contraction was necessary during your early development (it was a literal survival strategy), but it no longer serves you.

The main point to grasp in regard to this entire process is that when a stable entity with a contained identity begins to form mentally, emotionally, and somatically, boundless awareness (*what* you are) appears to become shrouded with *conceptual* limits and boundaries (*who* you are). Your true nature of boundless love and light *seems* to become progressively more shrunken with the auto-suggestion of your acquired subconscious beliefs.

As I have been saying, there's no one "doing" this consciously; "sleepiness" is the thread on which all the personal states of consciousness are strung. Thoughts in general (and the I-thought in particular) have an incredibly hypnotic quality; their movements mesmerize the innocence of attention like a snake charmer. This hypnotic process is really quite simple, though it is not easy to dispel once the hypnosis has taken effect! Through an unconscious or absentminded process of entrancement that continues well into adulthood (and is only dispelled upon awakening), awareness continuously assumes the apparent shape of the I-thought and the somatic self-contractions associated with it, giving rise to what feels *very powerfully* like a solid, separate self. In reality, however, this self that awareness assumes is nothing but an empty holographic composite. The shape of this composite identity is "assumed" in both senses: falsely adopted (or "put on" like a costume or posture) and unverified.

> Self-inquiry is a process of verifying the credentials of the separate person you believe yourself to be.

This tendency of attention to fall asleep or become hypnotized is why meditative traditions place so much emphasis on strengthening *attention*. When you are attentive, you are awake and dreamless; when you are sleepy, dopey, distracted, or dispersed, you're asleep and suffer nightmares.

I know it may be hard at first to accept that most of humanity literally walks through life in a hypnotic trance. Is it possible for people to do things like run companies, drive cars, go to work, and manage banks in a literal state of hypnosis? Yes, it is. In the same way that someone can sleepwalk at night—perfectly navigating the house, going to the fridge, eating food, and then safely walking back to the bed again—the condition of being a separate self is an "automatic" or "autopilot" state where functional activities can and do run smoothly. It's a habit-state, and habits run automatically like a machine. Only the *unconditioned awareness* is free to act spontaneously, without reference to the binding, deterministic chains of biological and biographical memory.

> While the I-thought is conditioned and determined, awareness is free.

Awakening Is a Natural Process

The conceptual personal identification and resultant sensation of separation from "the external world" constitute the core wounding of the psyche; together, they are essentially the core psychosomatic trauma that becomes the primary basis of all suffering. The reason for this is that, quite simply, it hurts to feel separate. The separate self is a dynamic of fear and desire, of neediness and lack.

However, it's important to note that *this core wounding is not a mistake.* The formation of ego is a natural, unavoidable developmental stage in the process of human maturation. All growth requires some amount of pain and wounding. It only becomes problematic when you *stop* growing at the stage of ego-development (as most people do), in which case you begin to suffer. It is healthy and ideal to evolve from being self-conscious to being self-aware. Most people, especially in the West, are not even aware that there are further developmental stages, remaining perpetually at the level of self-contracted ego-identification. Awakening consists of evolving beyond sophomoric states of consciousness into deeper, more expansive, even boundless regions of your being.

> Awakening could be described as an evolutionary shift from being a thought-based entity to an awareness-based nonentity.

Rather than being a rarified state of achievement, which is the way it often sounds, *awakening is a completely natural process.* Awareness wants to fulfill its deepest potential for self-knowledge in everyone in the same way that every flower has the urge to unfold and bloom simply because that's its nature; all the flower needs is the right combination of conditions, and it will bloom. The blooming of awakening essentially entails a process of softening and unfurling all the petals of self-contractions at the mental, emotional, and somatic levels. In the natural state of rest and relaxation, all your egoic defenses fall away, leaving only the openness, innocence, and freshness of your true nature like a bud that has fully flowered.

No matter who you are, this potential for awakening exists in you. And don't worry, after awakening, your "I-thought" still pops up, but it is no longer at center stage; it's merely conventional. You see and relate to it as a tool that's useful for practical functioning but not to navigate the world of self-knowledge in the truest sense.

Awareness Has No Location

One of the best ways to dispel the illusion of containment that the I-thought produces, thereby starting to "bloom" into the boundless awareness that you truly are, is to try to find the limits of awareness that you assume are there. While the I-thought apparently has a location in the head, awareness has absolutely no location. *Thoughts appear to be private and localized, but awareness is universal and nonlocal.*

Because of the process of ego development that I described above, you may have come to believe that awareness is "looking out of your eyes," but awareness is not directional like the physical light from a flashlight (going from the eyes "outward," for instance). Awareness would have to have some physical properties to have a direction like physical light. The conscious light of awareness isn't anywhere in particular. This is why I called awareness an "uncreated light" earlier; the light of awareness is shining ubiquitously in this moment, yet it has no dimensions in space and time. To be considered "created," something has to have at least one dimension. The realization that awareness has no physical, objective qualities helps prick the bubble of apparent containment and limitation. Let's try a guided meditation to explore this point experientially.

GUIDED MEDITATION: Trying to Find the Limits of Awareness

Material things have a beginning and end. They are measurable. However, that is not the case with awareness. Since it does not have any created qualities, it can't be "inside" your head. You can never "find" awareness the way you find, say, a set of lost keys or even an organ in the body. In this guided meditation, you will try to find awareness. Trying and *failing* to find awareness unravels the false limits that have been placed on your true nature.

1. Sit or lie down comfortably.

2. Relax all the muscles in your entire body. Soften the muscles in your head and face, especially the ones around your forehead, temples, and eyes.

3. Simply notice that awareness is present right now, lighting up your experience. You do this, as with the last meditation in the previous chapter, by *being aware of being aware*.

4. If awareness had a point of origin, like the light from a flashlight, you would be able to locate it. Try to find an origin for awareness in your direct experience right now. Is there an origin inside or outside your head?

5. Now, try to find not just the *origin* of awareness but awareness itself.

6. Notice that you can place attention on your body, but you cannot place attention on awareness because it does not have any objective qualities.

7. Can you notice that while your *body* begins and ends somewhere, awareness does not?

8. Now that you have discovered experientially that awareness itself has no created qualities despite the fact that it is lighting up your experience, contemplate awareness as an "uncreated light" for three to five minutes.

It is astounding to realize that awareness has no location in space and time. At first, the mind may come up with many objections and doubts. But the more you stick to your experience and not to your mind's interpretation, the more you will feel the joy and ease associated with your boundless nature as the "uncreated light" of awareness.

Some Blind Spots

There are some assumptions you may have about awareness that are so deeply ingrained in your ways of thinking, even or especially in spirituality, that it would be wise to point them out in this context.

The Myth of "Within"

Many traditional meditative techniques often reinforce the sense of spatial location particularly in reference to the head, which as we have seen is wrongly assumed to be the origin and location of awareness.

Some examples of practices that can perpetuate the sensation of separation include mantra repetition, closing the eyes in order to "go within," and even focusing on the "third eye" in the center of the forehead. I'm not suggesting that these things shouldn't be done or that they are innately "bad" or "wrong"; I'm only pointing out that they are capable of creating blind spots where the belief in and felt sensation of separation thrive. Left unnoticed, that is, they may strengthen the sense of an "inner" awareness and an "outer" world. They are a consequence of wrongly imagining that the "inside" of the head is a kind of hollow sphere or container where the knower lives. The physical light at the back of the eyelids when they are closed during meditation supports the impression that the mind is a hollow sphere or a literal space "inside" the body.

There are also many platitudes that can subtly maintain a sense that awareness is "inside" you. For example, since you may have heard that "The truth is within you," you may have an assumption that you're "in there" (inner space), that the world is "out there" (outer space), and that you need to "go within" to find truth. You may also have heard the question, "What is looking out from behind your eyes?" When you realize that awareness has no limits, however, you realize that you don't have to go "within" to find your true self and that awareness does not shine out of your head like the light from a lighthouse. The myth of "within" also lends itself to "private" experiences and aberrations, even "spiritual" ones, which are not ultimately the point, as you will come to see.

No One Has More or Less Access to Awareness

Another blind spot consists of the tendency to view some people as more awake or aware than others—as having more "access," somehow, to awareness itself. If you *start* from the perspective of containment, then you will inevitably project that structure onto "others." You will think of some people as deluded and others as enlightened, placing yourself somewhere on that imaginary hierarchy—probably very far down. Most people have incredibly deep feelings of self-doubt and even worthlessness, giving them the largely unconscious impression that they aren't good enough to be awake like the enlightened teacher they most admire and whom they put on a pedestal.

I am offering an absolute perspective here that can be quite shocking since most people are so accustomed to giving their power away to their teacher in big and in small ways, but this is an important pointer that can provide you with the trust and faith in your own self rather than projecting the power of awareness onto others, however illustrious they may be. I'm not suggesting that you should be egotistically self-confident; true self-confidence is the essence of humility (though not of *false* humility) because it's based on a realization of the absence of a separate self and the universality of loving awareness.

I'm also not dismissing or diminishing the importance of teachers; on the contrary, they are invaluable because without them, we would not receive the priceless message regarding the potential for our own awakening or the loving support we all need in the beginning. For this reason, it is entirely appropriate to have profound gratitude, love, and respect in our heart for our teachers.

At the same time, any authentic teacher will always remind you that *you* are the point and will tirelessly encourage you to discover your own divine identity rather than making you feel "less" than him or her in any way. The ultimate compliment to any true spiritual teacher is to go beyond the need (or the *neediness*) for his or her help.

The confusion often stems from the fact that some spiritual teachers have powerful energy fields, which can give the impression that they have more access to awareness than you do. If you have ever been around an awakened being, you have possibly felt an energetic resonance or even a deep sense of "transmission," and that can be very beautiful and inspiring. However, the perception that some people are more or less aware, more or less "transmitters" of awareness, or more or less "awakened" or "enlightened" *is precisely the bubble that needs to be pricked sooner or later.* That perception is dependent on the myth that awareness is contained inside your head and that some people have "more" of it than others. It is a dualistic *mis*perception.

> No one has more access to awareness in the same way that no particular fish in the ocean has more access to water.

If you start from your experience as boundless awareness rather than from the myth of containment, you will see nothing but the same radiant, wide-open, ubiquitous awareness "inside" and "out." Since awareness has no dimensions in space and time, it cannot be "transmitted" from "here" to "there" (or, as in the case with most seekers who feel separate from awareness, from "there" to "here"). Only something created can go from one place to another. Relative *energy* can be transmitted, and in that sense, relative transmissions do occur. It's important to make this distinction in order to avoid mistaking energetic phenomena for awareness itself. Awareness itself isn't limited to or dependent upon special yogic experiences, powers, or achievements. Because it is boundless, awareness is literally unconditionally open and available. Over time, this understanding infuses you with tremendous, even unshakeable self-reliance so that you can truly "be a light unto yourself," to use the Buddha's famous words to his disciples at the very end of his life.

Having said that, it's important not to abandon the teacher too soon, as that can delay or even prevent the full flowering of genuine awakening. There should be a natural falling away when the time is right and you are ripe—though that need not necessarily take long.

Awakening Signals the End of the Psychological Identity

Awakening from the trance of containment and separation fundamentally liberates you from the false psychological identity that has developed from infancy onward. The illusion that awareness is contained "inside" your head gives rise to the belief that you have a personal psychology based on the story of your life, the one that refers to and revolves around the I-thought that we discussed earlier in this chapter. Later in this book, in the chapters dealing with the shadow, we'll honor and integrate the relative psychological complexity of the human condition in the interests of balancing the absolute and relative points of view. For now, though, it's important to begin with a radical, even absolute understanding of the true nature of boundless awareness in order to cut right through the psychological identity cleanly, allowing you to flow in life immediately with more spaciousness, ease, and joy.

When you awaken to the absolute perspective, you come to see clearly how the illusion of containment, particularly in relation to thinking, produces the vast majority of your suffering; the thinking process, which is largely compulsive for most people, creates extreme discomfort due to being cooped up in such a small space. It goes round and round like a caged animal, kicking and screaming. All the commotion gives the impression that your thoughts, and the psychological identity they create, are solid and real. This is the realm of neurosis, narcissism, insecurity, compulsion, regret, anxiety, depression, worry, projection, paranoia, and fear. When you believe and become identified with your thoughts, particularly your I-thought, you really feel like you're "in there," that you are at odds with the world, and that there's something wrong with you. You will feel in the grip of psychological self-consciousness and will be under the impression that your true nature of boundless awareness has become eclipsed. But when you wake up to the absolute perspective, you realize that awareness can't be confined within anything or "eclipsed" because it has no limits. Awareness is naturally boundless and free, and like the sun, *awareness never becomes eclipsed from its own perspective.*

Something in you is roaring to be un-contained. Nothing in nature likes to be contained because containment is unnatural. That's why an animal will rebel when you put it in a cage, kicking and screaming for its innate freedom. Life is bursting with freedom. It's the boundless energy that makes a flower grow through a crack in the pavement, makes trees bountiful with fruit, and prompts life to procreate ceaselessly. So your system naturally kicks and screams when you feel that your identity is contained in the cage of the head. We try to stuff boundless awareness into a tiny space and wonder why we feel isolated, anxious, lonely, and needy. Suffering is nature's way of indicating that your way of experiencing is not in alignment with reality, which is fundamentally relaxed, spacious, open, and free.

Un-containing your thoughts helps relieve suffering enormously. When you realize experientially that thoughts arise in boundless awareness rather than in the painfully limited sphere of "your head" and that thoughts are not in fact "yours," their heaviness and potency are diluted; a thought becomes a small anonymous fish in a limitless ocean rather than a big fish in a small pond. You can begin to make this shift by noticing that awareness contains all thoughts, but no thought contains awareness. Awareness, therefore, is always "bigger" than any thought. You can also practice this shift by noticing that thoughts arise in awareness along with anything else you perceive such as the trees, the sky, the clouds, and the distant horizon. Your field of perception includes *everything* you experience. In fact, everything you experience (both "externally" and "internally") is "inside" awareness!

The realization that awareness is free, and that you *are* awareness, signals the end of your psychological identity. The entire convoluted realm of the psychological identity begins to evaporate like a mist. You no longer live there. With this approach, therefore, you *begin* with the realization that you are already the unconditionally open awareness that you have been seeking. You only need to notice the fact of your boundlessness by directly seeing your mistaken view of subjective containment, which gently clears up a general sense of confusion that leads to acute states of misery. Rather than trying to clarify the confusion on the level at which it was created, it would be wiser to replace the false perspective with the very fullness of seeing your mistake. The seeing of the false, which is synonymous with experiential insight, is all that needs to be done; it is the primary factor of awakening.

Awakening Reveals True Self-Love

It's important to note that this absolute, transpersonal understanding does not *deny* your humanity but *enlivens* it. On the contrary, the belief in separation cannot help but result in gross to subtle forms of inhumane behavior. When you awaken, your humanity actually becomes worthy of the name. The state of being a separate self inevitably leads to gross or subtle forms of cruelty, violence, and exploitation—in short, to *in*humanity. It's an insatiably desirous and fearful state that functions at an animalistic or even reptilian level. Since awareness knows no "other," it's bound to treat all aspects of itself with a holistic intelligence that naturally honors universal values such as kindness and decency. This is the true meaning of "self-love" and the foundation for compassionate service.

The evolution beyond an ego-based identity to presence-based awareness also does not mean you lose your unique personality; it simply means that you're not identified with it and that you see it with a healthy perspective. Without seeing your personality from a healthy perspective of boundless awareness, there will always be a sense of personal limitation either with a deflated or an inflated ego. Either way, genuine self-love will always elude you. With a deflated ego, there's a sense of worthlessness. With an inflated ego, there's an overcompensatory sense of worthiness. True self-love resides in the presence of awareness, which is beyond the limited dualistic concepts of "worthy" and "unworthy." Awareness contains all opposites, but no opposite contains awareness.

With this approach, you don't end with self-love; you start with it. I define "self-love" as the absence of separation. In that original state of wholeness that you began your life with, your presence or beingness is love itself, unconditional and free. Without the sense of separation, in other words, all that's left is the natural love of your pure and innocent being. It is important to understand that you won't ever *acquire* self-love for the simple reason that you *are* self-love; you have simply mistaken yourself as something other than that. Once you discover that there is no separation in awareness, true self-love will have been revealed.

A Quick Review

In this chapter, I explained the process of ego-development and made an important distinction between the I-thought and aware-ness. While the I-thought appears local and contained, awareness is nonlocal and free. By coming to understand how your separate sense of self developed from infancy onward and by seeing the process of ego formation objectively, you can start to disentangle your self from all the limited conditioning you have acquired and ultimately from your psychological identity. You can also start to settle into the self-love that you truly are. This process of un-containment may take some time, but it need not take long. The guided meditation in this chapter, where you tried and failed to find the limits of awareness, could even have triggered an immediate shift in you. If not, keep at it with heartfelt earnestness. In the next chapter, you will come to see how the seemingly external, independently existing world is based on an illusion of the senses with the I-thought at its center. You will also begin to discover how the world, rather than being passive and inanimate, is actually *within* creative awareness.

CHAPTER 4

THE POWER OF CREATIVE AWARENESS

In chapter 2, you became aware of awareness, while in chapter 3, you learned how the idea of an "external" world arose in relation to the idea of an "internal" sense of self. In this chapter, you're going to build on those realizations and push them even further. The point of this chapter is to awaken in you a mystical perspective on creation, breaking down the idea that the universe exists passively and independently of creative awareness.

For the sake of clarity, there are two perspectives that we have been considering: the conventional and the mystical. The conventional perspective sees material process and mechanically causal relationships. As I stated previously, it works very well at the level of practical, utilitarian, and scientific endeavor, but it does not offer *meaning* or *purpose*. The mystical perspective sees the aliveness, beauty, and timeless perfection of things as they are and honors the evolutionary impulse in life toward awakening. It works very well at the spiritual, emotional, and somatic levels, offering the meaning, purpose, conscious creativity, love, joy, and freedom that the human heart yearns for.

I invite you to consider the mystical pointers in this chapter with an open mind and heart. Since they challenge the prevailing modern Western assumption that the world exists independently of awareness, they will almost certainly rattle your belief system and worldview; they may even trigger deep existential, precognitive fears. Although they may sound incredible and even downright crazy from a conventional perspective, they are actually within your direct experience and quite easily verifiable from your own perspective. I ask only that you trust *yourself*—not me or anyone else. When it comes to freedom, you have to be willing to take full responsibility for the world in which *you* live and not rely on what you assume might be true in your absence or for someone else. After all, it's *you* who wants to be free. Do not believe what others have told you. Go by your own direct experience and experiment anew until the limited conceptual bubble in which you live bursts open into the reality of boundless love and light. Ultimately, as you will discover in chapter 6, you will have to go beyond all experience since *the absolute reality is trans-experiential*, but in the beginning, you must rely on your firsthand experience until you are able to go beyond it altogether.

The Mystical Perspective on Creation

From the mystical perspective, the universe does not have an absolute first cause, meaning that it did not begin objectively in the past as a one-time event that you are now perceiving as an independently existing phenomenon. That's the prevailing modern conventional view based on what I have been calling "scientific materialism": the dualistic belief that the universe is "out there," that it's made of material components that exist independently of conscious perception, and that it began in the distant past as a singular objective event. The conventional perspective sees life as inanimate, cold, random, and meaningless. It doesn't feel good. When you look with the singular eye of wisdom, however, you see and feel experientially that the universe is born and dies every moment with each fresh sensation and perception—and that it is conscious, self-aware, and intentional. From the mystical perspective, the universe is love incarnate. It feels blissful, both the pleasant *and* the painful parts. The mystic knows that the universe begins now and now and now and now...eternally. As Vincent van Gogh's painting suggests, which I discussed in the last chapter, *the universe is alive in this moment with conscious sensing and perceiving.* This is why some of the ancient tantric texts refer to you as God. Similarly, when Jesus said that "you are the light of the world," it could be argued that he was not speaking poetically; my own feeling is that he was referring to our identity as conscious light, which literally illuminates the world as an experience. You are the infinite potential of creative awareness in its expression as conscious perception.

> You are not living in the universe; the universe is living in you.

When the mystical perspective that I'm describing in this chapter began to awaken in me experientially, I started to experience the blissfulness of conscious perceiving at a deep neurological level. I even started to experience synesthesia as my senses blended together. When you awaken to the singular source of all experience and no longer feel separate from anything, the sharp conceptual lines separating the senses can break down or fall away, allowing for an intimate flow of experiencing where you are turned inside-out: your "outside" literally becomes your "inside." For me, this intimate rawness of sensing and perceiving was felt most acutely with color; to this day, I can *feel* color, especially the color of flowers, leaves, moss, algae, and grass—all of which appear to me extremely bright, like the light from illuminated neon signs, and feel blissful in my entire body. I also started to feel swaying grass and rustling leaves as though they were the hair on the back of my neck, the water in streams as though it were the blood coursing through my veins. Quite simply, the mystical vision of creation is ravishing.

The Universe Has No "Outside"

This may sound a little heady, but stick with me. In order to begin grokking the main pointer in this chapter regarding the power of creative awareness, consider the possibility that your only experience of "the universe" or "the world" consists entirely of knowledge in the form of thoughts, sensations, and perceptions. You have never experienced anything outside them; they *are* your experience. There's a major, truly radical implication to this statement that may be difficult to accept at first because of acquired beliefs and a particularly stubborn habit of perception, but it's a simple observation and essential starting point for self-realization: *in the absence of thoughts, sensations, and perceptions, there is no universe for you.*

Let's consider for a moment the idea that "the universe" is a really big "thing" or "collection of things" that exists "out there" objectively. If the universe were objective, it would have finite limits. It would be measurable. However, no one has ever found a limit, edge, border, or boundary to the universe for a very simple reason: there's no limit to whatever this is. If there *were* a limit, what would be on the other side of it? A really big space? Even a "really big space" is something. The Wizard of Oz? But that would be something, too! You would have to step "outside" of the universe to know or measure its limits objectively, but you are incapable of doing that because there's no "outside" to what we call "the universe." This realization is the full experiential import of the ancient mystical statement that "God is a circle whose center is everywhere and whose circumference is nowhere."

> From a mystical perspective, what we call "the universe" is an infinite or limitless subjective experience of awareness.

It must become clear mentally, emotionally, and somatically that, instead of being a separate person looking out at or passively observing an independently existing world, the universe continually arises and subsides in *you*—not you in *it*. Of course, by "you" I mean awareness.

The belief in an independently existing universe is an illusion based on an incredibly seductive, awe-inspiring illusion of the senses. *The word "illusion" refers to whatever appears to be solid and continuous in space and time.* Of all the forms of knowledge, perception is primary because it literally creates the world as an experience and makes it seem solid. You may object to the suggestion that conscious perception *is* the world; you might believe that although *you* may not have an experience of the world, others do. You may believe that the world is there whether it's consciously perceived or not. But that would be an assumption that you would never be able to verify first-hand. If you are not consciously perceiving something, for all intents and purposes, it does not exist for *you*. *If you can accept the simple experiential fact that awareness is literally creative, you will be free of the major obstacle to self-realization.*

Nothing Ever Happens

If you give primary reality to "the world" as an independently existing objective fact, you will always feel at the mercy of objective events—in other words, like a victim to whom things *happen*. To become truly free, you must come to understand that you actually have the ability to walk in and out of the world; if you did not have that capacity, you would be its prisoner. You start to access this freedom when you realize that, in reality, "events" and "situations" don't happen objectively; in fact, they are entirely created and shaped by your subjective point of view. This realization has an incredibly liberating consequence: *You are free to create and destroy how you experience the world.* The key is your *attention*. When you place your attention on something, it blooms in your field of awareness, and you will experience it as real. But you are also capable of turning your attention *away* from something, in which case it will wither and disappear altogether from your field of awareness and will cease to be an experience for you. That is your creative power!

When non-dual teachers say something like "nothing ever happens," they mean that nothing ever happens objectively or in an absolute sense. They are speaking from the mystical perspective of having understood the projecting power of awareness and having learned to turn their attention away from the inessential. These statements can appear ludicrous from the conventional perspective, but the more you wake up and see how awareness creates experience through a mixture of perception, memory, and imagination, the more you realize that you are independent of the world rather than dependent on it. You can then start to become free of all the limiting ideas and beliefs that you have projected onto yourself.

The Illusion of Space and Time

The illusion that space and time are objective, independently existing phenomena rests on the belief that the world is solid and continuous and that it's spread out in a linear line of time. Let's address each belief separately.

The World Is Not Solid or Constant

The conventional perspective normally assumes that the world is objectively solid and continuous, but when you examine your actual experience, you discover that the world is not at all solid or continuous. The world comes and goes all the time. The world gains an *illusory* sense of solidity and continuity from the presence of awareness in the same way that a movie gains the illusion of solidity and continuity from the movie screen. It is because *awareness* is ever-present that all your changing, discontinuous perceptions of the world appear solid. When you and I look at the world, the conventional perspective is that we are looking at the same world. From a mystical perspective, however, we don't share a common world; we share a common awareness. Our perceptions are altogether different and cannot be shared—each life form, in fact, lives in a unique universe—but awareness is the same in all cases because it has no limits. We make conventional *agreements* that we're looking at the same world for practical purposes, but awakening entails going beyond the conventional perspective in order to wake up to reality. You can still make conventional social agreements and live a totally ordinary life after you wake up!

Linear Time Is a Construct

The belief that the past exists on the left side of an objective line of time is deeply embedded in the structure of the way we think. Most people really do believe that the past is "back there" some-where, that things really did happen in a linear way. But the experiential fact of the matter is that the mind plucks out certain highly selective *memories* and constructs a narrative that seems to substantiate a linear perspective. We do this collectively with the narrative of history with humans at the center and individually with the story of our lives with "me" at the center. However, if you closely examine your experience, you will see how this trick works.

Take, for instance, the year 1989. First of all, everything that happened then is altogether gone. We are left with collective memory. Now, could you ever possibly account for *everything* that happened in that year? Imagine the incalculable number of events that happened with the weather, the billions of people, the totality of environmental and astronomical occurrences, the countless animals and insects, and so on. Nevertheless, if you were to read a history book, it would appear that certain things happened at certain times. The narrative would appear definite. But all narratives are based on *highly selective incidents* that do not reflect the infinite texture of every possible experience. There are, in fact, an infinite number of relative narratives that could be constructed depending on point of view. There's no such thing as an "objective" narrative. All narratives are relative, subjective constructs.

Instead of trying to imagine the unimaginable number of events within the span of an entire year, try imagining the number of events happening at this very moment. It's impossible! Everything always happens all at once—in "the eternal now," as it were—and only appears to be happening in a line of time when you start to pluck out certain highly specific moments and to fabricate a narrative that revolves around the sense of "me" at the center of experience. This false center has no actual existence, so the apparent events that are artificially constructed are revolving around a self that doesn't exist!

It really is interesting and revealing to apply this pointer to the narrative of your life, the one your thoughts repeat over and over again. Instead of telling yourself and others the familiar narrative of your life in which you focus on the usual incidents that seem to make up your identity in time, try remembering entirely different memories from your past in order to construct an altogether different narrative. I'm not suggesting that you make up events; choose actual memories of past events but just choose ones that you normally don't include in the story of your life. If you often tell a sad narrative, for example, try selecting only the good parts and telling a narrative based on those memories. Doesn't the narrative depend entirely on the memories that you select and shape into the collective memory of a personal identity? The more clearly you see this truth, the more you see the speciousness not only of your personal narrative, but also of the collective human narrative, and the more you are free of their dictatorial influence over your life.

The Creative Power of Sight

The illusion of an externally existent world rests largely on the sense of sight. When the eyes are open, there are no "gaps" in the visual field, which is primarily why the world *appears* to be so absolutely solid and independent. The sense of sight generates perhaps the strongest, most powerfully bewildering illusion of solidity, continuity, and permanence. It's a truly awesome magic trick. There are also biological reasons to consider, as there are many more neurons devoted to visual processing than to touch and hearing, taking up much more of the brain's cortex. These biological facts related to visual processing largely explain why you may retain the deep belief that the world is "out there" despite your lack of firsthand evidence; for example, you may believe that the world is still visually there when your eyes are closed or when you are in deep sleep. In fact, using the guided meditations in this chapter and the common daily experience of deep sleep as a big clue, you can begin to understand that "the world" is actually a discontinuous network of thoughts, sensations, and perceptions held together in awareness by the "crazy glue" of memory and imagination. There's absolutely nothing continuous about thoughts, sensations, and perceptions.

GUIDED MEDITATION: Feeling into the Discontinuity of Visual and Auditory Perceptions

When performing these exercises with visual and auditory perceptions, suspend for a few minutes your belief in independently existing perceptions and remain faithful to your heartfelt experience.

1. Sit comfortably and relax. Soften any tension in your body.

2. Now close your eyes gently for ten seconds. With closed eyes, do you have *firsthand knowledge* or a *belief* that the world is still there *visually*? Let your direct experience be your guide.

3. Now open your eyes, taking in the visual field for ten seconds.

4. Now close your eyes again for ten seconds, taking note of the fact that the world as a visual perception has disappeared. As a visual experience, it is discontinuous rather than continuous. Feel into your experience with intuition.

5. When you open your eyes again, can you notice that you are seeing *brand-new* visual perceptions that are being created instantaneously? The new visual perception has never been seen before in exactly the same way and will never be repeated. Every moment is a one-time event.

6. If you have the sense that you are seeing the same world, try shifting your gaze or position so you are seeing from a new perspective. Or consider how this moment is completely fresh, how everything has changed from one second ago: the Earth has moved on its axis and in its orbit around the sun, the trees have rustled, the birds have flown by, the clouds have shifted, your cells have died and been born, and so forth.

7. Now try to bring back the visual perception from one second ago. Can you bring it back as an *experience*, or is it gone forever, existing only as a memory?

8. Reflect on your experience.

Now let's try the same experiment with auditory perceptions. You will need to hear birds chirping for this exercise.

1. With your eyes closed, listen to the sound of a single bird or many birds chirping. Are the chirps "solid," or are they discontinuous?

2. Are you hearing the *same* sounds, or is each sound *a brand-new auditory experience*, never-before heard in exactly the same way and never to be repeated?

3. Cause and effect take time. Are the sounds arising in a causal manner, or are they arising *spontaneously* in "the eternal now"? Try to *feel into* the timeless quality of the sounds.

4. Are the sounds inanimate or animate in your experience? Are they dead or alive?

5. Reflect on your experience.

You can expand this exercise to include all sense perceptions. Natural sounds are more clearly intermittent than any other perception, so it's much easier with them to awaken to the reality of spontaneity, discontinuity, and emptiness. But since the belief in solid visual perceptions is particularly stubborn, I recommend performing the above guided meditation repeatedly until that belief is replaced by your direct, intuitive, heartfelt experience.

How to Embrace the World as Your Self

I am well aware of how strange, absolutist, or fundamentalist it may seem to suggest that the world does not exist independently of creative awareness, and I'm not denying the validity of the conventional perspective for practical purposes. At the same time, if your heart yearns for the total freedom that only awakening provides, you must be willing to go beyond the conventional perspective. The pointers in this chapter serve as a necessary station on your way to a complete understanding that ultimately does not negate the world but embraces it as a beautiful expression of the infinitely creative heart of awareness.

> Before you can embrace the world as yourself, you have to negate its independent existence.

There's a wonderful Zen saying that beautifully summarizes this process:

Before awakening, mountains are mountains and rivers are rivers; upon awakening, mountains are no longer mountains and rivers are no longer rivers; after awakening, mountains are once again mountains and rivers again rivers.

There's another marvelous saying that Ramana Maharshi used to point to the same truth:

Awareness alone is real.
The universe is unreal.
The universe *is* awareness.

Without the third element in both cases, the teaching would be lopsided and absolutist. However, the third element undercuts an absolutist perspective by dialectically unifying the other two opposing statements. They are both essentially saying that before you wake up spiritually, the world and everything it contains seems to exist independently. When you first wake up to the fact that the world does not exist independently of conscious perception, the world ceases to exist the way you thought it did; it becomes "unreal" or "illusory" as independently existing matter spread out in objective space and time. In the integrated stage that unfolds after awakening, the world still appears, but it no longer appears to be crystalized, inanimate, and objective; it is experienced as the momentary, dreamlike expressions of your true nature of boundless awareness.

A Quick Review

In this chapter, I made a distinction between conventional and mystical perspectives on creation. I invited you to consider and meditate on the creative power of awareness, replacing your belief in an objective, independently existing universe with your direct, heartfelt experience of its subjective nature. Hopefully you have begun to awaken to the experiential fact that the universe continually arises and subsides in *you*. The next chapter builds on the insights that you had in this chapter regarding the mystical perspective on creation. I will invite you to begin a process of self-emptying so you can experience the joy and freedom that come with the realization that you as the presence of awareness are independent of thoughts, sensations, and perceptions. By sifting out all the changeful elements of your experience, this self-emptying process will begin to restore the original shine, glitter, and radiance of your precious heart.

CHAPTER 5

INTERNAL POVERTY

Generally speaking, we are confused about what constitutes "wealth" and "poverty." We normally define those terms materialistically with a particular emphasis on monetary status. Simply put, we imagine that people are "wealthy" if they have a lot of money and "poor" if they do not. However, material possessions, or lack thereof, have nothing whatsoever to do with wealth or poverty in the deepest sense.

The Christian mystic Meister Eckhart has a marvelous sermon on this topic that played a significant role in my own awakening. In Sermon 52, Eckhart takes as his starting point Matthew 5:3 where Jesus states, "Blessed are the poor in spirit, for the kingdom of heaven is theirs." For Jesus, "the poor in spirit" are the wealthiest people of all. The question, of course, is what does it mean to be "poor in spirit"? To answer this question, Eckhart first makes a distinction in the sermon between "external poverty" and "internal poverty," suggesting that external poverty has its merits but that internal poverty must be understood in order truly to comprehend Jesus' statement. Although "external" and "internal" are relative pointers and must ultimately be abandoned, they are helpful for getting your bearings in the beginning. Once you turn away from the distractions of the world and turn your full loving attention "within," you will be able to meditate on Eckhart's main point: to be "poor in spirit" means to be free of all created things. As we discussed in chapter 1, attachment to created things breeds misery because they are impermanent; as Eckhart wisely suggests, freedom from the attachment to created things reveals the infinite wealth of peace itself.

The process of discovering your true self, of becoming "poor in spirit," consists of emptying out everything that was not original to you in order to understand through experiential insight that awareness is independent of its content. In the Christian mystical tradition, this process of discovery is called "the way of darkness" or the *via negativa* (the negative way). The technical Greek term for this process is *kenosis*, which literally means "self-emptying." In the nondual Hindu tradition, it's called *neti-neti*, which means "not this, not that," a similar process of discarding everything you are not. Based on these traditions, I'm referring to it as the "path of negation."

I know it may sound frightening to empty your self of everything you have come to identify with both externally and internally, but I can assure you from my own experience that it's actually a beautiful, loving process of cleaning out awareness to restore its original nature. Maybe you know how good it feels to get rid of clutter in your house or car. That goodness is incomparably more rewarding when you get rid of mental, emotional, and somatic clutter. You realize, "Oh, I don't really need this; I can toss it." It's a feeling of freedom, joy, spaciousness, and openness. There's an innate goodness in being empty. All the insanity of the human condition revolves around the clutter of mostly useless thoughts, particularly the I-thought and all the psychological craziness that revolves around it.

For maximum clarity, I have broken down this process of self-emptying associated with the "path of negation" into two parts:

1. This first part of this process, which is the subject of this chapter, leaves you empty of thoughts, sensations, and perceptions yet undeniably present and aware, breaking the spell that awareness is dependent on its content. This part essentially *de*-hypnotizes you by dissolving the false self you mistakenly took yourself to be and reveals the original radiance of pure awareness before it fell asleep in your limited identity.

2. The second part of this process, which will be the topic of the next chapter, will lead you into the realization that you are empty not only of thoughts, sensations, and perceptions but even of the experiential or conceptual sense of awareness itself. This second part empties you in an absolute sense, leaving only what I call "the uncreated reality" and resulting in true peace.

What Is the Self?

In order to begin the process of becoming "poor in spirit," I want to make some broad introductory statements that we'll spend the rest of this chapter examining and meditating on.

Let's first examine the notion of your "self," a word we use on a daily basis but generally don't know what it actually refers to. The word for "self" in Sanskrit is *atman*, which can also be translated as "soul," but don't let that term throw you; it's less abstract than you might think. In fact, the ancient sages meant by "self" exactly what you and I mean by that word in our normal, everyday usage: what we mean whenever we say or think "I," "me," or "myself." But what are the true qualities of the self?

First, your self must be stable and coherent; otherwise you'd have a multiple personality disorder! However, thoughts, sensations, and perceptions constantly come and go; there's nothing stable about them. How could random, ever-changing thoughts be your self? If they were, your self would be all over the place. In fact, only your conscious self is stable in relation to all changing experiences because it does not come or go, which is why you have the deep intuition of having a single, stable, unified identity.

Second, your self must also be that which is presently aware of your experience: the "I" that is conscious right now. The Sanskrit word for "consciousness" is *chit*, which has several meanings:

• The knowing principle

- To perceive

- To comprehend

- The animating principle of life

- Intelligence

In Hinduism, the term "atman" not only means "self" or "soul," but it's often used synonymously with "consciousness." *Simply put, consciousness is your self or soul.*

Again, that makes it sound abstract, but it's not; it's more concretely you than all the abstract *ideas* you have about your self as described on your curriculum vitae. Despite what you may think, consciousness is not conceptual and abstract. It is most tangibly appearing as your experience right now. Your separate thought-made self is an abstract idea, not consciousness.

I have chosen not to capitalize words like "awareness" and "consciousness" throughout this book because I want to avoid reifying them as proper nouns, mystifying them, and suggesting that there's some other kind of "extraordinary" awareness that you must acquire or strive toward or achieve. Rather than being stubbornly inaccessible or some "big deal" that only special yogis have access to, nondual awareness is unconditionally open and available. Most people simply do not realize the significance of what is already the case. The awareness reading these words is already extraordinary.

> Paradoxically, the shift that needs to take place is to see clearly that no "shift" into a "better" awareness needs to take place!

So, leaving aside the esoteric associations surrounding all these words, let us think of awareness in the most down-to-earth manner instead of as a lofty spiritual or "new agey" concept. It simply refers to your real self, that which is stable and presently aware. You can't help being that. You had no choice in the matter. You simply find yourself aware.

The Elegance of Ockham's Razor

Ockham's Razor is essentially a scientific principle of economy that empties out all unnecessary assumptions in order to arrive at the simplest, most elegant possible description or explanation of something. When applied to experience, the "razor" is so unsparingly sharp, as it were, that it "shaves" away literally everything except for the *only* thing it cannot shave away: the presence of awareness. When experience is present, you cannot shave away awareness because it has no objective qualities, but as we have seen, it cannot be denied since it's the fundamental ground of all experience—no awareness, no experience. Before you know *about* something, you simply know that you are present and aware. You know intuitively that "I am." It's irrational and even insane to deny awareness because you, the conscious subject reading these words, have to be present and aware in order to attempt to deny the presence of awareness.

> Relatively speaking, an assertion of its absence proves the presence of awareness.

As we saw in chapter 2, your conscious subjectivity is what separates you from a video camera or a robot, both of which lack sentience. You are able to experience and to understand the significance of what you experience. It's common sense that you are a conscious subject of experience. You are not dead or inanimate. Take a moment to verify these pointers for yourself. Ask yourself the following questions, pausing after each one for a few seconds:

1. Am I aware?

2. What is it that is aware that I am aware?

The answer to the first question is "yes," and the answer to the second question is "awareness." I, awareness, am aware. As you will come to discover in the upcoming guided meditation, the I-thought is not aware. Since it is *awareness* that is aware, your self can be said to have a self-aware quality. Awakening first requires you to be aware of the fact that *you, awareness, are aware*. It's an intuitive revelation of the self-evident fact of conscious being. Because awareness is subtler than the sense perceptions, it cannot be perceived, which is why it can only be known *intuitively*.

> You are not "aware"; you are awareness.

Self-Inquiry Is Scientific

When you asked yourself the two questions above, you were investigating your self scientifically. The path to becoming "poor in spirit" is not just mystical; it's also rigorously scientific insofar as you are applying the scientific method to your subjective experience in order to arrive at a first-hand understanding of the fundamental truth of that experience. This approach has been the backbone of Eastern meditative traditions for centuries; they refer to meditation, in fact, as a literal "science of mind." The reason for this is that you are applying your own first-person point of view in order to understand empirically your own first-person point of view. By this I mean that you know the presence of awareness *directly*, not as something other than yourself, precisely because it's the only self-evident and self-validating aspect of experience. It's known to you *as* you. Your self is closer than intimacy! It's what you *are*. You simply might not be aware that awareness, rather than the I-thought, is your self. Hence the need for scientific investigation.

In conventional science, this empirical approach is called the "scientific method" and culminates in reproducible results that support or contradict a theory. In spirituality, it's called "meditation," "contemplation," or "self-inquiry," and results in reproducible *insight* that similarly supports or contradicts a hypothesis with empirical evidence. In conventional science, you arrive at results independent of yourself, while in self-inquiry, you yourself *are* the results.

Keep the Change

Instead of amassing relative objective knowledge without knowing the actual knower of that knowledge, which is the norm, you seek here to know yourself as the one and only hard fact by which *all* things are known: the "I" of awareness.

As I suggested above, the presence of awareness is stable and coherent; in other words, it does not change in relation to ever-changing experiences. The knower of change cannot itself change; if it did, knowledge of change would not be possible. Just like the words on this page require an empty background that you rarely if ever notice when reading, all change requires a changeless "background." This background is the ever-present bridge of your true self between any two ever-changing thoughts, sensations, or perceptions.

In order to awaken to your self as the stable, coherent presence of empty awareness, it's helpful to use the changefulness or disconti-nuity of everything that appears as an *aid* to realization—as a reminder of what does *not* come or go. Changeful appearances reveal changeless awareness by *virtue* of their transience. Instead of being identified with and lost in a cacophony of changes, I invite you to notice intuitively that they point out your changelessness. While experiences are numerous and complex, awareness is single and simple. When you pay close attention to the changelessness of awareness that thoughts, sensations, and perceptions point out, you slowly awaken to the fact that you are awareness itself and not what you are aware *of*.

Since the psychosomatic self is made of ever-changing thoughts, sensations, and perceptions and blacks out altogether in deep sleep, it cannot be said to be solid and continuous. Just like the flowing frames in a movie give the illusion of solidity and continuity, flowing thoughts, sensations, and perceptions give the same impression. Belief in this illusion causes suffering because impermanence is the fundamental law of life, so whenever you try to fortify or grab onto an inherently empty, impermanent flow of experiences, you will feel a sort of "rope burn" as those experiences rush by you. When you examine the false egoic self closely, you discover that it's made of a discontinuous thought-flow (rather than being a solid structure) and that there is no solid entity *behind* the flow of thoughts.

Relating to the ego as a momentary "sensation" rather than a "structure" helps break down its apparent solidity. The ego is like a spider's web in the sense that it's filled with holes. The holes are the gaps between your thoughts, but instead of noticing the gaps, attention habitually gets stuck in the "sticky" filaments. Shifting attention to the discontinuity of the ego sensation helps clarify the confusion that comes with identifying your self with passing, incoherent states. You then start to identify more and more with the emptiness of awareness rather than with its momentary content.

When you say, for instance, "I am happy" or "I am sad," you create a verbal, grammatical confusion that conflates *what* you are (awareness) with *who* you are (your learned personal identity, the mask of your persona). "I" cannot *essentially* be happy or sad because those temporary states are changeful. When they disappear, "I" do not disappear. In between the momentary feeling of happiness or sadness, what are you? Your true self.

The realization that *I am awareness* and not what I'm aware *of* represents a profound, irreversible shift in understanding. Simply by changing your language, you can radically change how you experience whatever arises. For example, instead of thinking, *I am angry*, try thinking, *Anger is arising in me (awareness)*. This may not seem like a big deal, but it signals a fundamental shift from darkness to light. You can then begin to notice how awareness never actually gets stuck in the webs of identity that it spins out—in the same way that a spider can spin and withdraw numberless webs without ever getting stuck in any of them.

Concentration vs. Formless Attention

As a preparation for the following guided meditation, it would be helpful to make a distinction between concentration and formless attention. Concentration entails focus. We were taught in school to focus and strain in order to understand what was being taught. Because we "direct" it, concentration is acute and angular. It is relative to its object of concentration and hence dualistic. It also has levels and degrees of focus. Since concentration wavers, awareness must abide *prior to it*—not prior "in time" but timelessly. In other words, if you can be more or less concentrated, you are already there as awareness to make the function of concentration possible.

Instead of using concentration, which we often use as a kind of forceful and violent gesture, I will invite you gently and intuitively to notice awareness with your capacity of *formless attention*, which is an effortless, global, undivided alertness—an open, soft, all-encompassing wakefulness. It's a pure intelligence that's always here when experience is present.

GUIDED MEDITATION: Formless Attention

As an exercise to make this distinction between *concentration* and *formless attention* experientially clear, I invite you to try the following guided meditation. This is an important meditation, as I will invite you to employ formless attention later in the book on a number of occasions.

1. Take a moment to look up from this book, noticing that the entire viewing, whatever it is, appears readymade and whole in your field of perception. It's not divided up into parts. It's just one undivided visual perception.

2. Now don't concentrate on anything in particular. Just remain in a state of *formless attention* where you are globally aware of your entire visual field, including everything in your peripheral vision. You are simply awake and globally aware.

3. Now focus on one object and concentrate on it for five seconds. Then completely relax your concentration and dwell again in the state of *formless attention*.

4. Next, focus on that object again while simultaneously being *formlessly aware* of the entire visual field again. For example, if you focus on the tea cup, that doesn't mean the other objects aren't potentially in your peripheral field of perception. This step reveals how awareness can be aware on multiple levels simultaneously. This is a staggering realization that demonstrates the extraordinary nimbleness of awareness.

5. Now remain in the state of *formless attention* while moving your concentrated focus from one object to another. Can you notice how concentration is just a function of awareness and that awareness itself is its global context?

6. Now remain only in the state of *formless attention* for one to two minutes, globally aware but not concentrating on anything in particular.

7. Reflect on what you discovered.

Just to reiterate, the point of this guided meditation was to make it experientially clear that concentration takes place within an undivided, global, formless awareness that you rarely if ever notice because you're trained to concentrate on one particular thought, sensation, or perception after another. You are capable of being concentrated, formlessly aware, and both at the same time. You're trying here to "wake up" the *formless attention* and put it to good use, that is, to notice the effortless presence of boundless awareness that precedes the function of concentration.

Now that you experientially know the difference between concentration and formless attention, I invite you to try another guided meditation to practice the art of noticing that you as awareness do not come or go when thoughts, sensations, and perceptions come and go.

Before you begin this meditation, I would like to stress that "noticing" as I'm using it here is impersonal and impartial—not to be confused with "uncaring" or "indifferent," words that have cold, negative connotations that may signal aloofness or even denial. I'm not speaking of aloofness or denial here. On the contrary, this noticing is a form of *insight*, the only power that has the potential to dispel ignorance and to replace the pinch of suffering with the joy of freedom. It is a kind of gentle, compassionate emptying out of everything that is not original to you. It's essential that you remain as gentle and compassionate with yourself as possible. *Don't try to eradicate anything with strenuous effort.* If you are using effort, you will likely miss the point. Using the full range of your mental, emotional, and intuitive faculties, you're simply trying to understand your true nature as an act of self-love. You "pay" attention, then, as an act of loving devotion to your deepest self. When you engage in this inquiry as gently and compassionately as possible, with your best interests at heart and with great affection toward yourself, you begin to transmute the dense psychosomatic body into a more fluid field of energy and light.

GUIDED MEDITATION: Emptying Your Self of Thoughts, Sensations, and Perceptions

It is actually quite simple to empty awareness of all that is foreign or secondary to it by following some simple steps that are both logical *and* intuitive. The point of this exercise will eventually become so self-evident that you won't have to "practice" it any longer. You'll also wonder why no one ever pointed this out before. To perform this guided meditation, sit or lie comfortably. Take a few deep, conscious breaths. Soften and relax any muscular tensions, especially those in your head, chest, and stomach. Try to soften and then let go of your attachment to all the conditions of your life: for example, all your possessions, all your work and home responsibilities, all your roles, and all your relationships. All the things you let go of for purposes of this meditation will still be there when you are finished with this exercise. You are just taking a break from them for a few minutes to discover what you are for yourself in the privacy of your own heart. Take a few deep breaths and relax. Once you have softened and put down your attachments to the conditions of your life, rest there for a few minutes before beginning the following exercise. You will be employing your capacity of *formless attention* that you discovered previously.

1. While *thoughts* come and go, you, awareness, do not come and go. When a thought ends, you remain. Test this out in this moment by gently noticing with *formless attention* that you do not go unconscious when a thought ends. You (awareness) are ever-present in relation to ever-changing thoughts.

2. While *sensations* come and go, you, awareness, do not come and go. When a sensation ends, you remain. Test this out in this moment by gently noticing with *formless attention* that you do not go unconscious when a sensation ends. For

example, rub your thumb and index finger together, then stop rubbing them after a few seconds. Even though that sensation has ended, you (awareness) are still present and aware.

3. While *perceptions* come and go, you, awareness, do not come and go. When a perception ends, you remain. Test this out in this moment by gently noticing with *formless attention* that you do not go unconscious when a perception ends. For example, close your eyes for a few seconds, then open them. In between the two visual perceptions of the world, you (awareness) are still present and aware.

4. Now, remain in a state of *formless attention* without focusing on any specific thought, sensation, or perception. Try this both with your eyes open and with them closed. Dwell in this state for as long as possible, especially with your eyes open so you include the world in your meditation. This is a state of pure conscious love and light—your natural state of self-awareness. When your eyes are open, this is how a baby is looking at you and how you looked as a baby. Now, however, you have the added depth and wisdom of awakening that lends an unshakeable strength to your soft innocence.

5. If your attention gets "stuck" on a thought, sensation, or perception while you are in the state of *formless attention*, gently and lovingly withdraw it and remain formlessly aware again.

6. Are you as *formless attention* coming or going, or are you shining immutably despite the fact that the content of awareness is changing continuously?

7. Can you intuitively sense how you as formless awareness are inherently empty of thoughts, sensations, and perceptions?

You may have to perform these exercises many times at first, but as with anything, they do become easier with earnest, heartfelt practice. As you gently and lovingly continue to sift out all the changeful thoughts, sensations, and perceptions and simply notice with formless attention that *you* don't come or go—or that you are immutably present and aware in the gap between any two thoughts, sensations, or perceptions—you will come intuitively to realize yourself as the empty "remainder" of awareness itself. You are simply being pure awareness every time you notice that you are not something that comes or goes. *In the attentive noticing of what you're not, you're being "poor in spirit."* Keep repeating the meditations above, resting in that state of "internal poverty" for as long and often as possible.

This "empty remainder" of pure, formless awareness has been the only constant element in your life. For example, if you were to look at old photo albums of your life from childhood to the present, what's the only common denominator? The formless presence of awareness. Your body-mind has never been the same from one day to the next, not even from one moment to the next. But awareness has always been the same. No matter what was happening at any moment of your life, no matter where your body was, no matter how old you were—awareness was always shining formlessly as the total scene that appears in your pictures! When you look at your old pictures, try identifying with the formless awareness that lights up the *entire scene* rather than just identifying with your particular body. Notice how radically that changes your perspective on your life.

Freedom from Karma, Destiny, and Reincarnation

Being "poor in spirit" is extremely healthy; it fosters mental clarity and emotional intelligence. Normally, people identify with every inner state that arises, which creates a highly unstable, cluttered inner environment. By noticing thoughts, sensations, and perceptions without identifying with them, you remain consciously stable as the changeless, coherent factor of awareness, resulting in more natural spaciousness, ease, love, and wellbeing.

Internal poverty also radically changes your relationship to conditioning. Only something with form can be conditioned and in the grip of destiny. In a sense, karma and destiny are synonymous. Karma literally means "action," and simply put, it refers to psychological, emotional, and physical conditioning: past action produces the seeds for present action, which in turn produces the seeds of future action. Whenever you feel that "you" are compelled toward mental, emotional, or physical action, you are confusing awareness with conditions and experiencing the results of karma. Karma is actually an objective process of creation, preservation, and destruction. That process does not occur *to* a person; the egoic identity, being objectively observable, is itself part of the karmic process of creation, preservation, and destruction. Round and round it goes.

You are free of destiny when you realize that your true self, awareness, is not an object that can be compelled toward action. Your *thoughts* are conditioned and determined, but awareness is not. You arrive at this realization when you, awareness, notice that you can *see* your thoughts. *If you can see it, you cannot be it.* In the self-emptying process of becoming poor in spirit, you can only see what you are not. The more you notice your true position, the more the sense of being a person who is embroiled *in* this process diminishes because that which is embroiled *in* this process is seen to be the conditioned process of the person, not awareness. The apparent identification of awareness with *what* is known (and the resultant dysfunctional state) will eventually weaken, thin out, or snap, allowing boundless awareness—and the relative aspect of the uniqueness of your innate human personality—to function spontaneously, free from the neurotic self-criticism of the conditioned superego. Little by little, your natural state of space, freedom, love, and joy become more self-evident.

> As soon as you, awareness, can bear the appearance of the false separate identity without identifying with it, you are consciously free.

A Quick Review

It is my hope that this chapter gave you the practical tools to empty your self of thinking, sensing, and perceiving and to experience the joy and freedom that pervade the state of "internal poverty." By learning to sift out the changeful objects of experience from awareness as a devotional act of self-love, you have begun the process of dis-identifying with the false self that you have believed yourself to be. Ideally you were left even for a moment or two as the simple presence of awareness in a state of formless attention, of pure conscious love and light. As long as you have at least a basic intuitive grasp of the main pointers in this chapter, you are ready to move on to the next chapter, which will empty you even further. In the next chapter, you will learn how to empty your self of the experience or concept of awareness itself. In that state of absolute poverty, you will be at total peace and will be ready to explode from the boundless heart of awareness into the totality of relative experience.

CHAPTER 6

THE MOST INTIMATE POVERTY

As we saw in the last chapter, to be "poor in spirit" is to be empty of all created things. However, Meister Eckhart goes even *further* in Sermon 52, suggesting that "the most intimate poverty" consists of absolute emptiness and detachment where one does not even have the notion of being an empty self in which God could will anything. That is, if you were empty of everything created but still retained a subtle belief or concept that you had an empty self through which God could do something, then you would still not be truly poor in spirit. You would still be *full* of an "empty," "pure," or "special" self! Eckhart suggests very wisely that you must be empty of any landing place whatsoever, including of the idea of no-self or even of "God," which are themselves created notions arising after the uncreated fact of your true eternal being.

The purpose of this chapter is to apply this pointer to the presence of awareness, the fundamental ground of experience that we have been exploring throughout this book. In the last chapter, I suggested in the section having to do with Ockham's Razor that when applied to experience, the "razor" is so unsparingly sharp that it shaves away literally everything except for the *only* thing it cannot shave away: the presence of awareness. I stated that you cannot shave away awareness because it has no objective qualities but that it's simultaneously the *only* aspect of experience that cannot be denied. This is true *in relation to experience,* but in order to become truly free, you must be willing to let go of your attachment to awareness itself. Although I have used words like "awareness" and "consciousness" throughout this book, therefore, these are the final concepts that need to be emptied out—"shaved away," as it were—because they are a landing place. The purpose of this chapter is to leave your true nature innocent of *all* ideas and landing places, including non-dual ones, which will reveal the wealthiest state of all. This realization will replace your created sense of self—even your sense of an empty self called "boundless awareness"—with that which eternally abides as the absolutely changeless reality of all your relatively changing experiences. The good news is that this is the final step in the self-emptying process. You can't go beyond the uncreated reality. Nothing can.

I know it may sound dark, scary, and even nihilistic to empty your self of literally everything, but I can assure you that when you realize that you are absolutely uncreated at the core of your being, you will find your self pervaded by an unspeakable love and joy that you will never find in the realm of created things and experiences. Your heart will feel absolutely free and at peace, what Philippians 4:7 from the Bible describes as "the peace that passes all understanding."

Because the material in this chapter may seem highly abstract and conceptually challenging (despite its simplicity), I end the chapter with three practical, skillfully constructed guided meditations specifically designed to trigger this experiential insight on every level of your being, including and beyond a felt level, rather than allowing it to become abstract, theoretical, philosophical, or intellectual. Please keep in mind that what I'm pointing to is actually very simple.

The "I Am" vs. the Uncreated Reality

Before we go further, it might be helpful to distinguish between the two levels of reality that I am attempting to discriminate between in this chapter—and that we'll spend a lot of time exploring with practical guided meditations. The two levels are as follows:

1. **The created sense "I am"**: the bare experiential sense of conscious presence

2. **The uncreated reality**: the non-experiential, non-conceptual, eternal core of your being

The "I am" is a common term in mystical literature for God. It simply refers to your basic sense of conscious existence, which is the first and purest creative emanation of the uncreated reality. When you were in a state of *formless attention* in the last chapter, that was the "I am." It's just a state of pure conscious being. The dawning of consciousness is a godly, miraculous state because without the sense of conscious presence, no experience would be possible (and experience is nothing if not miraculous). However, strictly speaking, even the sense of conscious presence is a passing state. It appears and disappears like any other experience. This is why reality cannot ultimately be equated with experience, "knowing," or even "awareness" or "consciousness" as such. All experiences come and go, including the experience of conscious presence, while the uncreated reality does not.

We all experience the truth of this pointer every night when we fall into deep sleep (or when we go under general anesthesia), during which time the self-referential sense of conscious presence disappears altogether. In fact, if you watch closely, you can witness its disappearance every night at bedtime and every morning when you wake up. Since it's not always there, it can't be part of your "original face." There's a Zen koan that points in this direction: "Show me your original face before you were born." Since the sense of conscious presence certainly wasn't there prior to your birth, it can't be essential to what you are. Ultimately, your "original face" is whatever your bare sense of conscious presence vanishes into. I will invite you to see your "original face," so to speak, using the guided meditations in this chapter as a sort of "mirror." Ideally, when you look in this mirror, you won't see any image whatsoever.

> It is not wise to reify awareness or consciousness in any way.

There's a great Zen koan that is meant to trigger this realization: "Everything returns to the One. To what does the One return?" In other words, everything returns to boundless awareness, and boundless awareness itself returns to...the unnameable. The true answer to this koan cannot be formulated, as it is non-cognitive and, strictly speaking, non-experiential.

The Uncreated Reality Is the Negation of All Experience

Although I referred to the uncreated reality as "the core of your being," it's actually *right here*. It's not any distance from you because it *is* you. You are simply overlooking it by focusing entirely on gross or even subtle experiences. Because most people are addicted to experiencing, they won't let themselves acknowledge, let alone fully accept, the utter *simplicity* of their true nature. The mind loves complication; it revels in it.

In fact, it is precisely *because* the uncreated reality is so simple, unassuming, and humble—so completely innocent even of the barest experience—that it's so easy to overlook. Many people on the spiritual path imagine that self-realization has to announce itself in some spectacular experiential event, the spiritual equivalent of a psychedelic fireworks show accompanied by the Boston Pops playing in the background. However, the point to be grasped is that any-thing created in the form of experience—even a spectacular "spiri-tual experience" with flashy lights and a choir of angels singing in the background—will come and go in the uncreated reality. Despite the fact that the mind will likely interpret it as "boring," the uncre-ated reality is really what you're looking for because it is peace itself, the relief from the itchy desire for mundane or even spiritual experi-ences. *In this process of absolute self-emptying, it is precisely any form of experience that you are not.*

Searching for a created experience causes agitation rather than revealing the simple peace that abides here, eternally. As I pointed out in the first chapter, it is not wise to desire anything created because all created things are impermanent. *This includes any form of experience, spiritual or otherwise.* It is only truly wise to desire the eternal, which is the "final desire" that comes to an end once you realize that you *are* the eternal and only mistakenly took your self to be some-thing in space and time.

Letting go of all created things, even for a few moments at a time, is extremely difficult for most people not only because of attachments and addictions to experiencing that I mentioned above, but also because of attachment to one's psychological or even spiri-tual self-image. But it's a necessary stage in order to wake up from the dream of existence. In the next chapter, we will experientially investigate the generative and fruitful side of reality, but in this chapter, we're investigating the uncreated aspect in order to discover the wild, absolute freedom when you're not identified with anything whatsoever.

What we call "enlightenment" or "awakening" consists of the stunning intuitive realization that before you think, feel, or even sense that you exist, you're already there.

Preliminary Pointers for Awakening to the Uncreated Reality

Before I present the three guided meditations, I first want to offer some important preliminary pointers that will hopefully clarify what you're looking for, so to speak, and how best to look for it.

There Is Only One Gap

In the following exercises, I invite you to become the gap between your thoughts, between bird chirps, and between clock ticks. Even though it may sound like I'm talking about three different gaps, it is important to understand up front that it is *the same gap* in all three cases. There is only one gap! It is the uncreated reality at the core of your being right here, right now. It is the heart of being. It's important to know this so you can gather all your love, energy, and attention and place it on this one point—that is to say, on your self.

Be the "Unknowing"

It is also important to understand, at least as a working theory, that the uncreated reality does not "know" it is, at least not in a conventional manner. It simply *is*. This *is-ness* must pass from the realm of theory to direct realization for true freedom to emerge. It must be grokked with a *non-sensory form of knowledge*, which can paradoxically be thought of as "unknowing." The fourteenth-century Christian mystical text called *The Cloud of Unknowing* points in this direction. It is impossible to conceptualize or express a "non-sensory form of knowledge" or the "knowing of unknowing"; I can only point there with paradoxical phrases that make no sense to the mind and invite you simply to be the unknowing. Then you are ripe for the ultimate discovery.

The following guided meditations are meant to render you permeable to the uncreated reality by allowing your known or created experiences ("thoughts," "bird chirps," and "clock ticks") to subside back into your unknown and uncreated self. In this process, you ignore the known and allow your self to be the unknowing. You will have to get the feel for this kind of thing. It will take some practice to get used to being the unknowing instead of being identified with your relative knowledge and experience.

Relaxation Is the Key

I want to stress the importance of relaxation in this process. Eckhart suggests that you need to "break through" in order to realize the uncreated reality, and while there is some truth to this pointer, my feeling is that it's easily misunderstood because this process is not a willful, assertive effort. It's not like you're "breaking through" a wall with a sledgehammer to get to the "other side." What I discovered is that it's more like a breakthrough in terms of surrender. It's more like a break *down*. It involves dissolving the conceptual "wall" rather than breaking through it. It entails *relaxing, softening,* and *melting* all the self-contractions, ideas, and concepts back into the uncreated reality, into that pure state before they arose. I can't stress enough how important relaxation is in this process; if you tense up in any way, you will likely miss the point.

To facilitate the relaxation necessary for these meditations, I suggest that you do these exercises first thing in the morning, before you have had coffee, tea, or any other stimulants that increase thought-activity. These pointers are extremely subtle and are difficult to intuit when the thinking process becomes overly stimulated, which tends to snag your attention.

Set Down Your Worldly Concerns

You don't have to sell all your stuff and move to the Himalayas to become "poor in spirit" or even to discover "the most intimate poverty." All you have to do is put down all your worldly concerns for the time it takes to perform these meditations. Let the world run itself for a while. Again, you are not getting rid of your relationships, responsibilities, and possessions; you are just softening your "internal" attachment to them and setting them down for a few minutes at a time. It helps to perform these meditations, therefore, when you are not likely to have any interruptions or demands on your time and attention from "external" conditions.

Take Your Time

It's important not to rush through these exercises. Do one at a time, allowing each one to penetrate your mind, heart, and body. I recommend that you leave twenty-four hours between each meditation. Sleep on it. Let the body-mind rewire in accordance with whatever insights are revealed.

GUIDED MEDITATION: Becoming the Thought-Gap

Earlier in this book, I invited you to perform a guided meditation in which you first watched the flow of thoughts and then rested in the gap *between* them. Now that we are in a deeper context, I would like to offer a more subtle pointer. Instead of merely *watching* and resting *in* the gap between your thoughts, I'm going to invite you to be and rest *as* the gap. This is a significant distinction: *in* versus *as*. You are shifting here from *noticing* the gap (and hence being separate from it) to *being* the gap. The most powerful thing you can do to wake up to the uncreated reality—and to accelerate the evolution of consciousness in the relative sense—is to be conscious without thinking and then simply to *be* the gap between your thoughts. Doing this even for a few seconds at a time is extremely potent— even though you may not be aware of its effect in a self-reflective or cognitive sense. Just doing this meditation, whether or not you are aware of its effect, begins a process of purification that will continue over time without any effort on your part.

1. Sit or lie down comfortably. Rest the body-mind without becoming drowsy or falling asleep. Remain in a state of relaxed alertness.

2. Now gently place attention on the flow of thinking, noticing that when a thought ends, you are still present and aware.

3. Now gently ignore the thoughts themselves and notice, instead, the gap *between* each thought. Do this for two to three minutes.

4. Now *gently feel into the gap* with your attention and intuition so that you have a kinesthetic or felt sense of resting *as* and *being* the gap. Do this for two to three minutes.

5. What does it feel like to *be* the gap? Reflect on this for two to three minutes, resting the body *as* the answer to this question.

6. Now, as you continue *being* the gap, let go of the feeling, the intuition, or any attempt to describe or define the gap. What remains? Dwell here for at least a few minutes—the longer the better.

The main point of this meditation is to make it clear that passive "witnessing," which is a common technique in Eastern meditative traditions, is not enough to bring about a substantive shift in under-standing. You have to *become* the gap between thoughts and actively stay there for at least one or two moments at a time. This gap is the literal source of life and consciousness; it's where "the juice" can be found since its potential is infinite. Because passive witnessing never enters or activates the gap, witnessing can seem dry or boring and may even lead to an existential apathy, malaise, or gray dullness, basically a desert of monochromatic detachment. It lacks heart and vitality. Many people with whom I work report feeling this way because of the practice of witnessing. Repeatedly placing attention on and then actively *being* the gap—even for brief moments—heals the wound of separation over time and allows your true self to func-tion integrally again.

Terminology Can Become a Trap

Ideally, your answer to the final question in the previous guided meditation was wordless. If any word came to mind or any percep-tible experience arose, it was not the final answer. Don't allow your self to land anywhere. To leave reality unformulated is the most radi-cally honest—and the single most difficult—thing for a human being to do precisely because it's a non-doing; it entails *refraining* from formulating a definition of your self. Most people are so addicted to "doing" that they cannot fathom "non-doing." Thoughts will pop up to try to fill in the gap. They are remarkably seductive. Just notice and gently disregard this tendency to name or understand what you are. The point of non-duality is not to leave you with the most pro-found ideas and concepts about life but to live outside all frames of reference. Otherwise terminology can become a trap.

So when you realize that you *are* the gap between thoughts and the thought arises, *Oh, that's what I am!* (or something like that), gently notice and allow that thought to vanish in you just like any other thought or feeling. In the beginning, there must be a supreme vigilance with such thoughts because they will unconsciously rein-force the separate sense of self in the form of a "spiritual ego."

GUIDED MEDITATION: The Soft Center of Experience

Now that you have done a guided meditation in which you became the gap *between* your thoughts, I invite you now to become *the same gap* but this time in relation to what I call the "soft center" of experi-ence, the empty space that receives all perceptions. Paradoxically, the "soft center" is "soft" because it's empty, and it's "rock solid" because it's immovable. For this guided meditation, you will need to sit in a place where you can hear the sound of a bird chirping.

1. Sit or lie down comfortably. Rest the body-mind without becoming drowsy or falling asleep. Tune in to the sound of a chirping bird.

2. Now ignore the sound of the chirps, gently placing atten-tion on the emptiness (or "soft center") into which the chirps vanish. Do this for two to three minutes.

3. Gently feel into that space so that you have a kinesthetic or felt sense of *being* the soft center. Rest *as* that space.

4. What does it *feel* like? Reflect on this for two to three minutes, resting the body *as* the answer to this question.

5. Now, as you continue *being* the soft center, drop the felt sense of it and do not conceptualize it in any way. What remains? Dwell here for some time.

The more you keep feeling into and resting *as* the gap between thoughts or the soft center, the more you will *feel* like no-thing instead of merely believing it conceptually. You can do this throughout the day with any sounds that arise, but I will say that chirping birds have a special place in meditation; they have awakened many a Zen master. There's something divinely creative about birdsong. It's the soundtrack of nature and has a special ability to affect radical shifts in perception and identity at the head, heart, and somatic levels. As always, it's the mental, emotional, and somatic *feeling* of your self as no-thing that's truly liberating. When this understanding remains only mental, it actually creates a layer of concepts over the "soft center" that does not allow the *actuality of the experience* to enter directly into your empty being, which is why some people may "intellectually" understand non-duality but still *feel* like a separate self. It's like placing a nylon tarp over your garden, pouring water on top of the tarp on a daily basis, and then wondering why the flowers aren't growing. Just like water can't penetrate nylon, truth can't penetrate your being through the tarp of ideas, beliefs, and concepts.

The Eternal Presence

"The eternal presence" is another term for "the uncreated reality" at the core of your being. The eternal presence, however, is not the same as "the present moment" (or "the now") as popularly understood because passing experiences have no substance of their own. By the time "the present moment" has been experienced, it's already the past. How can a passing experience be considered real? The present moment appears and vanishes so quickly that you can never actually grasp or even find it. It's altogether momentary and derives its appearance from a timeless factor: *you.*

So while "the present moment" is experiential, "the eternal presence" is non-experiential. The present moment is a split-second flowing experience, while the eternal presence is the subtle eternal background of all experience. The eternal presence is not a moment *in* time; *it's the timeless factor behind or underneath two ticks of the second hand on a clock.* To use a simile, the eternal presence is like a riverbed, and time is like the water flowing through it. The riverbed, of course, does not flow.

As with the gap between your thoughts and the "soft center" between the chirps of a bird, the eternal presence does not come or go the way thoughts, bird chirps, and the ticks of the clock do. *It's always here as an is-ness.* While the ticks are created and give the impression of duration, the eternal presence is *uncreated* and has *no duration.* While the sense of conscious presence (the "I am") appears and disappears, the eternal presence does not. It is the absolute underlying reality that lends a sense of temporal "continuity" to all relative experience. It is what gives the frames in the movie of waking life and dreams a sense of flow and solidity.

GUIDED MEDITATION: Awakening to the Eternal Presence

As an exercise in shifting attention from *the present moment* to *the eternal presence,* I invite you to sit near a clock or wristwatch with a second hand that ticks audibly.

1. Sit or lie down comfortably. Rest the body-mind without becoming drowsy or falling asleep. Remain in a state of relaxed alertness.

2. Tune in to the sound of a ticking clock.

3. Now, instead of focusing or concentrating on the ticks, ignore the ticks altogether and gently notice with *formless attention* the presence *between* the ticks. Do this for two to three minutes.

4. Gently feel into the presence so that you have a kinesthetic or felt sense of *being* it. Rest *as* that.

5. Is the presence coming and going, or are the *ticks* coming and going?

6. Now try to notice both the presence and the ticks *simultaneously*.

7. Now, just rest *as* the presence again and then drop the conceptual, kinesthetic, or experiential sense of "the eternal presence." What remains?

As with the other two meditations in this chapter, you ideally awoke to the *is-ness* that cannot be named or understood conventionally. This process will initially take lots of practice, but it will eventually become so self-evident that no practice will be necessary. I suggest that you practice until the need for practice falls away naturally, like a piece of ripe fruit falls off a tree when it's ready.

The Power of Reality to Heal

The more you meditate on the uncreated reality, dropping anything perceivable or conceivable, the more nourished you will feel and the more healed your body-mind will become at the cellular level—not because you tried to attain those outcomes but because they are the natural effects of this contemplation. Waking up to the uncreated reality heals the body-mind of fragmentation and reestablishes its energetic flow. It is the source of the benevolent healing factor that constantly strives in all life for wellbeing, unity, integration, and love. These self-emptying exercises are the healthiest things you could possibly do for every level of your being.

If you could forget every other practice and simply be the gap, you would come to know beyond a shadow of a doubt that at the core of your being you are absolutely free, that your "I" refers to freedom itself and not to the personal self made of the intermittent "ticks" or "movie frames" of thoughts, sensations, and perceptions.

In fact, if you could just get a *glimpse* of the uncreated reality, you would never be the same again. It's that potent. Make it your home. Ground your body-mind in the truth of it. One drop of that blissful nectar can initiate a process of healing beyond your wildest dreams. You will stand in awe as you see the changes occurring in your life without any effort. *The only effort you need to make is to stop the effort of being what you are not.* Grace will take care of the rest. The more you give your heart to this endeavor, the more you will be guided and protected, nourished and healed.

A Quick Review

The purpose of this chapter was to reveal the infinite richness of "the most intimate poverty." You now have some tools that you can use to empty your self not only of thoughts, sensations, and perceptions, but also of the presence of awareness in an experiential or conceptual sense. Even if you only tasted one moment of the absolute freedom I was pointing to, you no doubt felt a tremendous relief. Once you know you are independent of all created things, you are free to express your heart as the undivided totality of conscious experience. In the next two chapters, you will walk the "path of inclusion" in order to see and feel your self as the beginningless and endless flow of life itself. You will learn to see clearly and feel deeply that reality is not only inherently empty but also the true substance of everything you experience. That is, you will come to discover and *feel with your whole being* that you are no-thing *and* everything that you experience, which can be described as the natural state of "empty fullness."

CHAPTER 7

INTERDEPENDENCE AND DIVINE VIBRATION

Imagine an ocean with numerous whirlpools. Each whirlpool has a shape of its own and is distinct from every other whirlpool. Each one also has a lifespan depending on conditions (if the weather or tide change, for instance, some whirlpools will be destroyed, while others will be created). From its own perspective, each whirlpool is separate from all the other whirlpools.

But from the perspective of the ocean, all the whirlpools, though unique and distinct, are made of the same ocean water. The ocean can be said to be whirlpooling, therefore, without ever becoming something other than water and without ever exhausting its ability to create numberless unique whirlpools. Ironically, the formless water is "invisible" to the whirlpools precisely because there's nothing "other" than water in their experience. The substance of their own being is "hidden" in plain sight because a form can only see other forms. A form cannot "see" the formless—though the formless is the substance of *everything* it sees!

Similarly, each body-mind is a whirlpool in the shoreless ocean of awareness. The ocean of awareness is "shoreless" because, as you have discovered throughout this book, it has literally no experiential limits, borders, edges, or boundaries. It takes on apparent boundaries when it whirlpools as what we define as "a body," but the *substance* of each body has no inherent form. A whirlpool is a shape and shapeless at the same time.

Ultimately, distinction without separation is what makes true relationship and love possible. Even though you and I are both whirlpools in the same homogenous ocean of boundless awareness, "you" are still "you" and "I" am still "I" for as long as the whirlpools of our bodies last; this paradox is the meaning and purpose of relationship— and why the uncreated reality appears to itself as a diversified field of experience. The point of life, if life can be said to have a "point," is to love, to be loved, and to be the flowing love between the two.

The main point of the whirlpool metaphor is to suggest that there's no separation anywhere in nature, though uniqueness and diversity are not only entirely natural, but also necessary for experience to arise. Basically, the aim of spirituality is to heal the unnatural sensation of separation that you have come to feel in order to restore your natural undivided state of fullness, joy, and conscious aliveness—in short, your innate freedom. The Buddhists refer to this freedom as your "birthright." Similarly, the word "yoga" means "to join or unite," the purpose being to join the body and the mind and then the body-mind with its radically free and unlimited environment, thereby replacing the separate sense of self with a universal one. All the yogas have unity and freedom from limitation as their goal.

The prior two chapters were a necessary precursor to this path of unification and inclusion. You first had to discover experientially that your self is the uncreated reality of all relative experience, including the felt sense of conscious presence. By highlighting the uncreated reality, you arrived at the experiential insight regarding "the most intimate poverty." However, the path of negation merely served the purpose of emptying you of the false center of experience so that you could be filled to the brim with the true boundless flow of nature.

In this process of inclusion, you will come to realize and embody the fact that you are not only the uncreated reality, but also the common source-substance of *everything* you experience. Accounting for the generative and fruitful side of the uncreated reality makes experience possible in a relative sense and ensures that reality is not static. You are empty and bountiful, still and moving at one and the same time. When the psychosomatic self has been removed or at least weakened through insight, life no longer bumps up and grates against a false center of experience. Conscious experience becomes an uninterrupted flow of energy without any separation between your body-mind and the boundless totality of nature.

In this chapter and the next, we'll explore your natural unity, fullness, and vibrancy both in a logical and, most importantly, in a felt sense. We'll do this by considering the nature of interdependence, "divine vibration," dream yoga, and perception. Instead of relating as a separate whirlpool to other separate whirlpools, totally asleep to the boundless ocean of awareness, I'll invite you to soften the rigid attachment to the name and form of the body and include in your field of awareness *the common formless source-substance out of which all the whirlpools are made.* The realization of your undivided, vibrant nature restores the conscious shine that you experienced in early childhood and have longed for ever since you have acquired the impression of having lost it.

The Law of Interdependence

"Interdependence" is a key pointer in Buddhism and a profoundly liberating one when it comes to breaking down the belief and felt sensation of separation. Interdependence is essentially a law of nature stating that all things are interrelated in a dynamic web of being without beginning or end. Everything "co-arises" in relation to everything else in an uninterrupted flow of interdependent relationships. In fact, change and flow are so totally ubiquitous that no separate, solid, independent "thing" ever forms except conceptually or imaginatively. For example, the whirlpool in our metaphor above never actually *becomes* a solid shape—although it does temporarily have a *relative* shape that makes it distinguishable and hence perceivable. It's actually made of water that's in constant swirling motion. We normally think of the body as a separate, solid shape that will die one day, but when you consider the body as interdependent with the environment and in constant motion, you come to see and to feel that, like the whirlpool, it never actually becomes a solid, separate object in the first place.

> The body is a purely energetic phenomenon that is coextensive with its dynamic environment.

At no point can you remove the body from its environment or freeze the frame. You can take a picture, but the picture will be a static representation and not the living reality. Not only is the body-mind not apart from nature; the body-mind *is* nature—just as the whirlpool *is* water. Boundless awareness is temporarily verbing as your body-mind, or any other form that you experience, just like the ocean is temporarily verbing as a whirlpool! The habit of thinking of the body-mind as a noun instead of as a verb produces tremendous fear and anxiety, particularly when it comes to the concept of death.

When you think about it, the sensation of being separate from nature is peculiar. For instance, we say things like, "I went for a walk in nature today," or "I love being in nature," as though you are one thing and nature is another thing that you have to *visit*. In fact, *nature goes for a walk in nature*. The conceptual division between you and nature rests on a severely limited sense of yourself. We could learn a lot from ancient traditions that have a more holistic, animated view of life—the Native American Lakota people, for instance, who view the Great Spirit (Wakan Tanka) as residing in everything.

Your Body Is Cosmic

Let's consider the human body at the level of biological interdependence. The average human body has approximately 37 trillion cells, and around three hundred million of them die and are replaced every minute. When one cell dies, the entire human organism continues to function; in fact, the very life of the body *depends* on the seamless, continuous death and rebirth of its cells.

> The body is a continuous process rather than a static product.

Furthermore, the average human body contains 100 trillion microorganisms, outnumbering human cells by a wide margin. Despite the fact that the human body is comprised of virtually countless human and nonhuman organisms working symbiotically not only in relation to the organism as a whole but also in relation to the environment, we imagine the body as a *single* organism wrapped up into a discrete separate package and labeled "me." But your cells and microorganisms didn't come stamped with your name on them; they are anonymous! In fact, life is anonymous. When you conceive of yourself as a separate and solid individual body, you will inevitably fear death, but when you know yourself as the infinite web of being and the boundless awareness that spins the web, you will know that *what is* can never die because it was never actually born. In reality, the apparently single organism labeled "me" never began the way you *think* it did; it just began *conceptually.*

When you realize and feel the interdependent nature of the total functioning, your action becomes spontaneous. Like all physical processes that are without dis-ease, healthy action sinks largely below the state of morbid self-consciousness. It's only when you don't realize the law of interdependence that you are painfully and unnaturally self-conscious in a psychological sense rather than naturally self-aware, which is a state of playful spontaneity.

To awaken to this spontaneity, consider how you are only ever conscious of a miniscule percentage of the total number of natural processes that contribute to the body's survival and activity. When you consider the astounding symphony of natural processes in the universe (or perhaps multiverse)—from the subatomic to the astronomical—it starts to dawn on you that the total functioning was *always* performing *all* actions, including those arbitrarily thought of as "yours." It was only a mental idea of separate agency that claimed conceptual ownership of them. If a whirlpool could think, it might imagine that it had separate agency. It might think, for example, *I am whirlpooling*. But that would be a mistake. It's swirling in accordance with the interdependent conditions of the total ocean. The *ocean* is whirlpooling.

Try sensing into how boundless awareness, nature, or the universe is thinking your thoughts and performing your actions, rather than a separate "I," and notice the difference in how you feel. Notice how expansive and relaxing it is, how much of a relief from the burden of having to figure life out and to get it right. When this false sense of personal agency thins out or disappears through insight, the natural state functions spontaneously *as it always did* but now without the conceptual irritation of separation that causes the discomfort associated with "personal" will, choices, and responsibilities—all of which have a density, heaviness, and seriousness to them. When you wake up, though, you simultaneously realize that there's no actual switchover; spontaneous, universal functioning was always the case, even when the "I-thought" gave the impression of control and separate agency.

The Limitation of Thought-Labels

The belief in separation stems largely from an illusion created by thought-labels. The Buddha taught that names and forms are "conventional designations" or "thought-labels" that serve a merely practical function for purposes of communication. The problem comes when you mistake conventional designations for reality, imagining that they refer to separate "things" that are really there independently of the total interdependent functioning.

Take a single blade of grass, for example. Within a boundless field of conscious experiencing, concentration plucks out and focuses on something that *appears* to have an inherent name and form: a blade of grass. But a "blade of grass" is a mental label for something that does not actually exist the way you *think* it does; it does not exist with its own "self-nature" (meaning that it does not exist independently or separately) because a blade of grass is *wholly dependent* on the earth, soil, water, sun, clouds, rain—in fact, on infinite causes and conditions because each of those causes depends on other interdependent causes. Without any *one* of those conditions, what we think of as a "blade of grass" could not exist. A blade of grass, therefore, is empty of a separate self because it's inseparable from a web of being that has no *actual* beginning, middle, or end. In other words, when you're looking at a blade of grass, you're looking at the boundless totality of nature!

This is also why a "blade of grass"—or anything that appears to have an inherently separate self—can be considered a "gross thought." *In other words, if you're seeing something that appears to have an inherently separate self, you're seeing through a filter of thought-labels.* The "trick" of the senses with the aid of thought-labels makes "things" seem separate and independently existent when, in fact, they aren't.

This is the true meaning of "emptiness" in Buddhism. Many people misunderstand what the Buddha meant by "emptiness," assuming he was referring to some kind of nihilistic void. But that is not the case. What he meant was that a "thing" is empty of an independent "self-nature" but full of totality. Emptiness and fullness are two sides of the same coin. As the *Heart Sutra* puts it famously, "form is emptiness, and emptiness is form." Once the uncreated reality manifests as experience, you can't have one without the other.

GUIDED MEDITATION: Attuning to the Interdependent Environment

Let's take a moment to consider this interdependent web of being in an experiential sense. This guided meditation is meant to awaken you to the fact that your body is literally coextensive with the limitless environment. This realization softens the tendency to think of yourself as a separate and isolated self, as an island of identity.

1. Take a moment to rest comfortably and to come into the felt sense of the body. Take a few deep, conscious breaths. Rest for a few more moments.

2. Now ignore your mental commentary and attune experientially to the fact that the oxygen "outside" the body is as much part of the body as any "internal" organ. It literally sustains the body and plays as vital a role as the heart and lungs. You *are* the oxygen because without it, the body would not survive. The lungs are being breathed by virtue of the oxygen that the trees are producing. The "inside" and "outside" are one integrated system and are only conceptually distinguishable for purposes of practical communication. Furthermore, oxygen itself is entirely dependent on trees, which are themselves entirely dependent on water, the sun, the Earth, the atmosphere, and the boundless space in which the Earth makes its orbit. There's no separation anywhere (though there is still distinction).

3. Now, as you breathe normally, become aware of and *feel into* the fact that the trees are extensions of your lungs. Feel into your physiological relationship with them. If you are a visual learner, you might consider imagining the oxygen as a vapor that you can see as it travels from the trees into your lungs, creating a direct link or bridge between the trees and your

body. Feel into how you are breathing in the oxygen that they are incessantly producing. Feel into how this is one single, integrated, organic process that is being done by nature. *The body is being breathed by life itself.*

4. Now contemplate the selflessness of the body, that is, how it's empty of a separate self given its interdependence with countless other factors.

5. For at least three to five minutes, consciously steep the cells of the body in the feeling that this meditation produces.

6. Reflect for two or three minutes on what you have discovered experientially.

Ideally this guided meditation produced a feeling of rest, expansion, interconnectedness, selflessness, and gratitude for nature and for the miracle and mystery of the body. When you investigate the law of interdependence carefully in the way we have done here, you come more and more to experience—mentally, emotionally, and somatically—that your body is coextensive with the limitless environment. In this sense, the cosmic body *is* your body. I don't mean this poetically or figuratively but literally!

Death Exists in Map-Land

In the last guided meditation, you felt into the body's relationship with the interdependent environment, ignoring the mental commentary that gives rise to the belief in and felt sensation of separation. You may begin to understand how relying on mental commentary in the form of "thought-labels" is chiefly responsible for the fear of death. Thought-labels can be considered maps in the sense that they are intended to help you get your bearings in a technical sense but are not meant to be your dwelling place. Perhaps another metaphor will help make this point clear.

There's an old saying that "the map is not the territory." If you were to look at a map of a country, you would have the impression that there were divisions between different states; you would have the feeling that one state "begins" here and "ends" there. But if you were to visit the territory itself, you would not find a natural separation between two states. For instance, if you were traveling in the United States, mainland Europe, or India, your experience would be of a single landmass. The different names of states, and the lines shaping and separating them, are purely conceptual, only existing on a map and not in the territory itself. "New York," for example, is a conventional name and form on a map rather than an inherently separate territory from the rest of North America. It only "begins" and "ends" somewhere because some people said it did on a map. Human beings may put up a wall or fence between two states or countries, but such a wall or fence would not be natural; it would be arbitrary and, in fact, most unnatural. Maps are meant to be helpful in the functional sense of getting your bearings. Once you get your bearings, you are meant to put the map down and go to the territory. You are not meant to live in Map-Land!

Similarly, your name and form are like a state's name and form on a map. In your case, the map is your conventional identity as reflected on your curriculum vitae, in your photo album, and on various governmental documents, such as your birth certificate and passport. However, you now know that you cannot find where you actually begin or end since your body is braided with the environment in a single interdependent fabric of experience. Like a country, life is a single "landmass" without inherent divisions. As we have seen, everything in life depends on infinite causes and conditions because every cause must itself have a cause. Every plank of wood in a house was previously a tree, which was previously a seed, which was previously another tree...and on and on.

And so it is with the body. In other words, there is no beginning or end to any chain of causation. It's only when you look at the "map" of your birth certificate that you have the sense of having "begun" at a certain time, and when you imagine the "map" of your death certificate, you will conceptualize a moment in time when you will have "ended." But these divisions of your apparent birth and death only exist in Map-Land. They are not actual. This realization is profoundly liberating and has the power to alleviate or even dispel the fear of death, which only exists in Map-Land and not in reality.

Appearance vs. Reality

The more you practice refraining from mentally labeling everything you experience (or at least not grasping onto or believing the thought-labels), the more you come to understand why the mystical traditions make a distinction between *appearance* and *reality*. The reality is *the timeless, boundless actuality of awaring,* and the appearance is based on all your mental *labels.* All labels are limited. The same holds true for what you imagine to be "your body" and anything else that you arbitrarily separate out from the totality with a thought-label.

Anything that you separate out from the totality will eventually disappear (if it appeared, it must also disappear), but the totality *of which it was never actually separated in the first place* does not itself come or go because it has no limits or boundaries. The totality is infinite and eternal; the seemingly separate part appears and disappears with a combination of the matrix of the senses, creative imagination, and mental commentary.

I am suggesting here that there are two modes or ways of experiencing. In the first, which is based on appearance, you experience life through the filter of thought-labels. You see separate, independently existing things. This way of experiencing diminishes what is in reality a boundlessly interdependent, active, spontaneously creative process into a limited, static, passive mechanism. This mode of deadened experiencing is responsible for the sense of boredom, the sense of repetitive perception, and the illusion of predictability.

In the second mode of experiencing, which is based on reality, you ignore the thought-labels and experience life directly *as the awaring (the common source-substance) out of which all experience is made.* The second type of experiencing is called seeing with the eye of wisdom instead of with the physical eyes. Merely relying on the senses and thought-labels gives rise to mirages and hallucinations (such as the belief "I'm going to die"). Most people tend to look at the world with a "blank stare," never really *seeing* anything, let alone *being the awaring.*

GUIDED MEDITATION: Being the Awaring

In this guided meditation, you will learn the new habit of dropping the thought-labels and intuitively knowing and feeling yourself as the formless awaring principle that is the common source-substance of all experience.

1. Sit or lie comfortably. Take a few deep, conscious breaths. Relax any tensions in the body-mind. Relaxation is the key.

2. When you are relaxed, look at something in your field of vision as though it's a "thing" that exists independently of your experience, something that's "out there." Think the thought-label for that thing.

3. How does that mode of experience feel? Reflect on this for a minute.

4. Then look at it in the second mode, with the eye of wisdom. To do this, *soften your concentration on the object and do not mentally label what you see.* This is what I mean by "being the awaring." It is a state of pure conscious light, the state of *formless attention* that you discovered earlier. Try this for one minute or so.

5. Now look around slowly for another minute. As you pan the environment, continue being the awaring. Notice that without mentally commenting on what you see, you as conscious light are shining without division, judgment, preference, or interpretation—*no matter what you're seeing*. Without mentally labeling things, the visual field is just one undivided field of conscious light. It's all lit up equally.

6. How does it feel to be the awaring rather than experiencing through a filter of thought-labels? Reflect on your findings for a few minutes.

In the first mode, you might have noticed how your mental labels create a haze of perception that makes things seem like separate objects and that makes you "like" or "dislike" them. However, when you looked in the second way, with the eye of wisdom, you hopefully discovered that conscious light actually shines equally on all experience without the divisiveness of mental commentary. Ideally, being the awaring was softer, gentler, more lucid, more awake, more all-inclusive, sharper, and more animated than the habitual way of perceiving.

Being the awaring will take practice at first, lots and lots of practice. It is difficult at first to relax the concentration on specific objects and refrain from mentally commenting on everything you see. If you do find that your mind comments, simply relax the commentary as much as possible and let those thoughts flow by without grasping onto them.

The Body Is Divine Vibration

The previous guided meditation can seem "cold" and "detached," so it's important to marry the spaciousness and neutrality of awaring with the qualities of warmth, intimacy, affection, and benevolent lovingkindness. This kind of practice should not result in cold detachment; on the contrary, the main point is to awaken the *heart*, which inexhaustibly pours its beautiful spirit into all of manifestation out of the overflowing generosity of unconditional love. In this section, it's vital that you energetically feel into these pointers and guided meditations with emotional and somatic resonance. It's *the emotional and kinesthetic sense of unity and aliveness* that has the power to transform your rigid habit patterns into more fluid expressions of true nature.

The tantric school of Kashmir Shaivism calls the energetic aspect of awareness *spanda*—"divine vibration"—to account for the animate, energetic, fruitful, bountiful aspect of the uncreated reality. "Divine vibration" is a marvelous phrase that beautifully captures the true nature of the body and of life itself. Previously in this chapter, you came to see that the body, like a whirlpool, is not a stationary object; it's in constant motion and is experienced primarily as vibratory sensations (and partly as perceptions). The body is not a solid "thing" that belongs to "you." The belief that the body is solid rests largely on the physical image of the body that you see reflected in the mirror, but that impression is based on a trick of perception; the body, of course, is changing all the time; it just *appears* solid because it's changing so slowly that you can't perceive the change in real time. If you could watch a time-lapsed video of your body over a period of twenty years, you would see that it's actually changing not only daily, but moment-by-moment. However, when you believe the *appearance* of solidity and claim ownership of the body, thinking of it as "my body," you will cling to it and fear its loss.

But when you ignore the appearance of solidity and tune into the actual *experience* of the body, which is made of ever-changing sensations and perceptions, you discover that the real body is more like an "energy-body" in the sense that it's made of vibration rather than solid stuff. It's actually a borderless field of vibrating experience. When the body is felt as the energetic vibration of many trillions of cells and microorganisms in a single symphonic harmony with a non-conceptual intelligence that spontaneously functions in relation to the interdependent web of being, the sense of the body as being solid and "mine" loses its grip and begins to fade away.

GUIDED MEDITATION: Feeling the Body as "Divine Vibration"

The point of this guided meditation is to awaken you to the boundless energetic, biological aliveness that you *think* of as "your body."

1. Sit or lie down comfortably. Take a few deep, conscious breaths.

2. Drop down and tune into the felt sense of the body, ignoring any mental images and focusing entirely on the energetic vibrations. Soften and relax. Rest deeply.

3. Notice any tingling sensations or cellular vibration in your hands, feet, or chest. If you feel tingling or vibrating anywhere, put all your loving attention on it. The tingling or vibrating is awareness dancing as pure aliveness.

4. Notice if you can feel your heart pumping or your blood coursing through your veins. If so, be the energetic pulsation of those sensations. *Feel your entire body as a cosmic nerve ending.*

5. If you don't feel anything, which is not uncommon for people who first begin this practice, try rubbing or clapping your hands together for several seconds, feeling into the warmth or tingling created by those movements. Also try gently and mindfully shifting around in your chair or bed so

you can feel the energetic sensations associated with that movement. If you are still having a hard time awakening the energy-body, another helpful method to increase blood flow and neurological tingling is to tap or pat your arms and chest quickly but *very gently* for ten to twenty seconds. The neurological aftereffect of that method usually feels like a pleasant "buzzing" sensation on your skin. Another technique is to put a hot water bottle or warm heating pad on your chest, feeling into the pleasure of the sensations. Yet another technique is to place your hand over your heart, feeling into the throb as it continuously pumps 1,500–2,000 gallons of blood daily in total service and devotion to life. Stay with any sensations once they have been activated in your field of conscious awareness.

6. If there are thoughts arising, you can relate to them, too, as divine vibration. They are awareness dancing as thought activity.

7. Notice if there is warmth anywhere in your body. If so, become aware of the fact (and thankful) that the body is alive. If you feel gratitude for being alive, or better yet for being *aliveness*, steep in this emotion for as long as possible. Gratitude is profoundly healing.

8. Now imagine that you are steeping the body in the felt sense of aliveness like you were steeping a teabag in a pot of hot water. Imagine the body diffusing into the space like the tea diffuses into the hot water. As the body diffuses into the boundless space, it's becoming less personal. Continue to steep for three to five minutes like a calming cup of chamomile tea.

9. After three to five minutes, reflect on your experience. How did it taste?

10. If the flavor was pleasant, savor the aftertaste for as long as possible.

Hopefully this meditation awakened the energy-body to some degree and made you aware of how pleasant it is simply to *be* and to regard yourself as divine vibration. The more you feel the body as the divine vibrations of creative awareness, the more the experience of life becomes blissful. Even if there's pain somewhere, the pain is a generic call from the loving intelligence of the system to signal the need for self-care and healing. Try softening the label "pain" and feeling into the sensations rather than resisting them. If there is no physical pain in the body, try feeling gratitude for that blessing. Feel the natural state of being as though you were receiving a big hug from Amma (known as the "hugging saint"). You might also begin to sense the omnipresent benevolence of being. It *wants* to heal and integrate—and to love.

A Quick Review

In this chapter, you contemplated the law of interdependence and the vibrational nature of conscious experience, breaking down the belief in and felt sensation of separation and solidity. The more you meditate on interdependence and drop into the vibrant reality of divine vibration, the more you will feel like the beginningless ocean of life itself. You will also discover the wellspring of nourishment that you were always looking for outside yourself. Consciousness in its expression as divine vibration is profoundly nourishing and healing. As that, you *are* the nourishment for which you were in search! The more you feel that nourishment as an expression of your very own conscious self, the more you are practicing self-love and are honoring your adorable nature as life itself. As you continue to honor yourself by resting in and as the natural state, the more the cells in the body are flooded with light energy. The cells literally start to tingle and vibrate with unconditional, benevolent love. They wake up! This cellular awakening is an important part of the process. The energy field of the body-mind becomes "transfigured" when you pour the warm nectar of your loving attention on it. Other people will also pick up on that healing energy without your having to say a word. They will be drawn to you. Self-love radiates and transmits at a subtle but powerful level. In the next chapter, we'll complete the "path of inclusion" with a contemplative exploration of dream yoga and with some meditative contemplations on the spontaneous, undivided nature of perception.

CHAPTER 8

DREAM YOGA AND PERCEPTION

In this chapter, you'll continue to awaken to the common source-substance of all experience the way you did in the previous chapter. Just to reiterate, the main point of this step is to awaken you to the fact that everything is *within* and *made out of* boundless awareness. In other words, the entire range of relative experience is your shimmering self-display because *it cannot be known apart from or outside of you.* If it were "outside" of you, the presence of awareness, it would not be a conscious experience, and if it were made out of something other than awareness, there would be two separate substances in your experience. However, through a series of guided meditations, you will come to realize how boundless awareness is the sole source-substance of all experience and that nothing is "outside" of it. Let's begin with a discussion about dream yoga and end with some contemplations on the nature of perception.

Dream Yoga

Even though many of us spend our whole life in denial of the fact, we all know on some level that life is a momentary dream. This notion appears not only in classic literature, but also in popular culture. For example, there's the 1955 song "Life Is But a Dream" by the classic doo-wop group The Harptones and even the classic nursery rhyme and popular children's song "Row, Row, Row Your Boat," which ends with the same line: "life is but a dream." These simple sentiments are powerful reminders of the astonishing brevity of life.

The pointer that life is but a dream also appears in ancient spiritual sources. It's one of the main teachings, for instance, in the *Yoga Vasistha*, a classic non-dual text of which Ramana Maharshi was very fond and one that he often recommended. In this text, the universe is described as "a long dream," and the sage teaches that both the dream and waking states are superimpositions on the underlying foundation of infinite consciousness just like water in a desert mirage.

In Tibetan Buddhism, there's even an entire form of spiritual practice known as "dream yoga," in which practitioners gain liberation by treating sleeping dreams and waking life with equal measure. The process begins with "lucid dreaming," which is where you are awake to the fact that you are dreaming *while you are dreaming*. You are lucid (aware or awake) in the dream. Becoming a lucid dreamer, both with nighttime dreams and with the dream of one's life, is a powerful practice that can break the spell of hypnotic, "sleepy" states of mind and that can reorient your perspective to include the world *within* your self rather than viewing your self in the world.

In this process, you wake up to the fact that whatever seems to be spread out in space and time is literally dreamt up as a momentary appearance. In fact, the sensation of duration *is* the dreamy sensation of existence—the sense of dragging on in time. This realization is especially helpful when it comes to thoughts and emotions, which can seem substantive and heavy when they arise. With dream yoga, you begin to relate to thoughts and emotions as insubstantial and dreamy—literal daydreams—rather than taking them so seriously. It's highly liberating.

The Dream State

Essentially, dream yoga teaches that daytime life is no different from a nighttime dream—or if it is, it's a difference in degree and not in kind. One is longer than the other and has different rules. In fact, from your own perspective, they are both intermittent and momentary; the waking state only *appears* to be solid, continuous, and independent because you have been conditioned to perceive, think, and feel that way. Let's first consider the dream state and then compare it with the waking state.

Imagine that you have a dream at night in which you are viewing a scene that includes a mountain. You will probably grant that in the dream, there are no objects made of inanimate matter that took time to develop but only empty, luminous awareness spontaneously appearing as the entire scene: the mountain, the trees, the people, your body, and everything else. There is no place in the dream where awareness ends and "matter" begins. In the dream, that is, there isn't awareness *of* a scene—it's not as though there are "real" objects in the dream that awareness beholds like a flashlight shining on something that's already there—but only awareness spontaneously appearing as the entirety of the dream. It's *all* awareness (including the space between all the apparent objects) with no limits or boundaries, no "inside" or "outside," and no "depth" or "shallowness." Every expression of awareness in the dream has *equal value* since it's nothing *but* awareness through and through. It's awareness both in essence *and* appearance. The entire dream is made out of you, the one who dreamed it.

The Waking State

Now, you might agree that the scene in your nighttime dream is an insubstantial, momentary appearance made of awareness, but argue that the scene in your waking state is "real" because you see it every day, not just as a fleeting appearance. However, the seeming stability of the scene in the waking state is an illusion created by memory and assumption. In fact, as you discovered in chapter 4 regarding the power of creative awareness, every moment is made of a brand-new perception that only appears to be consistent with a previous perception because you compare the reality of present experience with the memory of a past one.

If we just focus on the mountain for a moment, mainly because mountains seem so solid and permanent, we can explore the assumption of permanence. The idea that you can visit the same mountain over time, day after day, is a mistaken assumption created by a severely limited perspective of time. Let's say, for example, that you visited the apparently same mountain in your waking state every day for fifty years. From the perspective of a human being, fifty years seems like a long time, and fifty years' worth of viewings at 365 times per year would equal 18,250 viewings in human time. That would appear to be convincing empirical evidence for the solidity and permanence of the mountain. But again, it's an illusion of perspective.

To make this pointer clear, imagine you could watch a video of your visits to the mountain plus an extra eight billion years on a time-lapsed film that was sped up to accommodate the viewing in one minute. Would you see the same mountain? (It may be helpful to know that our own sun will die in roughly six billion years, swallowing the Earth in its phase as a red giant.) Would your 18,250 viewings still seem like a lot of evidence for the permanence of the mountain, or would the entire fifty years, which once seemed like a long time broken up by separate days from the *human* perspective, now seem like the blink of an eye? The solidity of "things" is an illusion based on the sum total of the flashes of perceptions—which turn out, from a cosmic perspective, to be momentary and altogether dreamlike. In fact, from the perspective of the eternal, the sum total of the perceptual flashes of the mountain over fifty years would be the fleeting equivalent of a single night's dream—at most!

The difficulty of seeing everything as awareness arises largely from habitual ways of perceiving, based largely on unconscious memory. Your experience is determined not only by conscious memories, but also and even especially by unconscious memories that have their roots in childhood precognitive development. Unconscious memory makes you think you know what you are seeing and that it's there independently of your seeing it. It's so deeply embedded in the structure of the psyche—it *is* the structure of the psyche—that it's difficult to deconstruct once it becomes formulated as the default program of experience. Through dream yoga, this program can be examined, brought to conscious attention, deconstructed, and replaced by conscious light—what Tibetan Buddhists call the "clear light" or "luminosity."

The Point of Dream Yoga

Dream yoga essentially gives you a healthy perspective on life, allowing you not to take things so seriously, to be more creative, and to have more fun. The point of this practice is not to produce a feeling of apathy, leading to the nihilistic question, "If it's all a dream, what's the point?" *The point is that life is so brief that every moment is precious rather than pointless.* You begin to spend your time wisely instead of frittering away what little time you have. If done correctly, dream yoga strengthens love and compassion because you see everything and everyone as an aspect of your self, so you are likely to treat everything and everyone with equality and respect and care, which are extensions of self-love in the universal sense. When it's all your own creation, you love it the way a mother loves her only child. Rather than producing apathy, which is possible if this teaching is misunderstood, dream yoga should produce feelings of peace, freedom, spaciousness, joy, and compassion.

By practicing dream yoga, you can also lucidly dismantle the habit of viewing the world as solid, "external," and limited. You can break down the attachment to your own body by seeing it as a dream object just like in a nighttime dream. Viewing your body in this way reduces the fear of sickness, aging, and death. You begin to feel the body, mind, and world *within* your self as a brief yet intimate creative expression of your deepest self rather than as independently existent, hostile, and threatening. You let go your grasp on it because you become awake or lucid to its inherent transience (and hence beauty) as an experience.

GUIDED MEDITATION: Lucid Dreaming in the Waking State

In this meditation, you will be invited to view your daytime experience as a dream appearing in and made of the common source-substance of awareness.

1. Sit or lie comfortably. Take a few deep, conscious breaths. Relax any muscular tensions in the body.

2. Once you are relaxed, become aware that you are dreaming the dream of waking life. This is called "lucid dreaming." You are aware that you are dreaming the waking state. You are awake in the dream of life—the "day dream," as it were.

3. Now, gently and lucidly look around at your surroundings, awake to the fact that everything you see, taste, touch, smell, and feel is literally *inside* you like a nighttime dream. How does that feel?

4. Now look at your own body-mind as a dream appearance that is appearing in the dream of awareness just like anything else. How does that feel?

5. Can you feel into how everything you are perceiving in the dream of waking life is within and made of boundless awareness?

6. Reflect on your insights for a few minutes.

Ideally, in this meditation, you felt that your entire experience was "inside" you and that thinking, sensing, and perceiving were literally made of awareness just like everything in the nighttime dream. If fear or anxiety arise in this practice, try not to identify with them. If you do identify with them, you have essentially stopped being a lucid dreamer and are taking your thoughts and feelings to be real; you are becoming absorbed in them the way you do with a dream (or a movie), asleep to the fact that it's a dream and that there's nothing really to fear. Try waking up again and lucidly relating to whatever is arising for you, both "internally" and "externally," as dream appearances.

It's also important to apply this practice of dream yoga in your daily life, especially in your relationships with other people. This practice lessens your reactivity to situations that normally push your buttons. When you interact with others as though they are inside boundless awareness and made of the same substance as your own body-mind, you tend to have more space and compassion in your life. You can see that when people are mean or unkind, their behavior comes from being asleep to the dream and taking life too seriously. In other words, it's important that you *feel* how all your experience is a dream arising and subsiding in the heart of awareness. If you feel cold and distant or nothing at all, you're probably dissociating from life, and that's not the point. Again, this practice should open your heart to your identity and oneness with all of life. In fact, dream yoga is really *a way of life* that takes daily and nightly practice. I'm just giving you a small taste of it here.

Spontaneous, Undivided Perception

I'd like to explore one last way to approach the "path of inclusion." This approach involves suddenly awakening to and consciously embodying the spontaneous, undivided nature of perception. We'll explore the spontaneous nature of perception first and the undivided nature of perception second. Although they are two aspects of the single boundless awareness, I have broken them down for purposes of clarity and to facilitate their experiential absorption.

Spontaneous Perception

In chapter 2, you became *aware of being aware*, which I suggested was your greatest treasure. Now that you have read more of this book and have had many insights about your true nature, I would like to share how to go beyond even *that* pointer so you can awaken to the diaphanous, spiritually brilliant conscious light that you are without any effort whatsoever.

The first point to grok is that awareness functions flawlessly when your body and mind are in a state of total relaxation. Although you may think that you have to tighten the eyes or scrunch the forehead in order to concentrate or to function in life, that is not the case. The reason you may think that is because you were most likely taught in school to contract, to "pull it together," in order to get things done. You were scared by your teachers into self-contraction, focus, and concentration. However, the senses function spontaneously and effortlessly without having to contract in any way whatsoever. In fact, it's unnatural to *try* to be aware!

GUIDED MEDITATION: The Diamond of Awareness

One of my favorite Zen sayings is by Hsuan-sha: "The whole universe is one bright pearl." Another translation runs like this: "The entire world of the ten directions is a single shining [or 'luminous'] jewel." This saying beautifully points to the fact that awareness is naturally self-luminous, that it shines radiantly in all directions, and that it's not in need of being perfected. Let's try a simple guided meditation that will make this saying, and the main point of this section, experientially accessible and clear to you. I invite you to notice how effortlessly, naturally, and spontaneously you function as creative awareness.

1. Sit or lie down comfortably. Take a few deep, conscious breaths.

2. Take a moment to relax all the muscles in your body completely, especially all the ones in your face. If there's any tension around the eyes, temples, or forehead, relax it as gently as possible—with as much gentleness as you would use to kiss a sleeping baby on the forehead.

3. If there are lots of thoughts, relax them as much as possible. It is not necessary that they stop altogether.

4. As the body-mind rests in a state of deep, total relaxation, notice that perceiving is functioning flawlessly without any effort whatsoever.

5. Are you, awareness, *trying* to see these words? Are you *trying* to hear the sounds that are arising? Are you *trying* to feel the sensations that are arising?

6. Notice how awareness functions spontaneously before you are even cognizant of it as an *experience*. For example, if you hear the sound of birds chirping, *the sounds are heard before you are even cognitively aware of the fact.*

7. Now simply rest as the natural state of spontaneous perceiving, without even being cognizant of it, for two to three minutes. There's no separate "you" who needs to "get it" or "awaken." Absolutely no effort is required now. You are in the ultimate state without effort.

8. Reflect on what you have discovered.

Hopefully this guided meditation awakened you to the fact that being boundless awareness does not require *practice*. It's the natural state! Without trying, you as awareness are "the animating principle of life," which you will recall is one of the definitions of *chit* (the Sanskrit word for "consciousness"). Awareness is like a diamond that is sparkling because that's its nature. It's actually easier than "easy" and more effortless than "effortless." It's already done. It's a gift. It happens without the efforts of the fictitious "middle man," which is why this particular awakening is not a question of "transformation" but of simply noticing what is already the case.

Going Beyond Aware of Being Aware

Tibetans have a marvelous word: *ziji*. *Ziji* means to be full of shine, glitter, radiance, or splendor. In Tibetan Buddhism, it refers to an inner quality of confidence and dignity that comes with the recognition of your inherently pure nature as the diamond of awareness. This recognition automatically shines and sparkles in your overall energetic signature, especially in your eyes and on your face. It is perhaps the quality that Jesus had during the Transfiguration, but it's equally available to you here and now. As the natural shine, glitter, radiance, and splendor of awareness become self-evident, a healthy confidence and dignity of action flow naturally.

The important thing to stress for our purposes is that *ziji* is not a quality that needs to be *cultivated*. It's already here as the reality of boundless awareness. You as awareness are already full of shine, glitter, radiance, and splendor! You are already spiritually brilliant conscious light. Absolutely nothing needs to change in order for this to be so. The confusion originally stemmed from the conceptual realm: "within" awareness, a whirlpool of an idea had formed that seemed to give rise to a separate "you" who needed to "get it" or "awaken." To remove that idea in the previous meditation, I pointed out how that was not actually the case. As I suggested at the beginning of this section on spontaneous perception, *this realization is one subtle step beyond the pointer to be aware of being aware.* At first, you were aware, but you were not conscious of the fact. Then, to initiate the awakening process in chapter 2, I invited you to become aware of being aware, which required a slight intuitive effort. Now you are waking up to the fact that what you are requires absolutely no effort, which could not have been realized without having gone through this process!

> In reality, that which you want to awaken, awareness, is already awake.

Undivided Perception

In this section, we'll build on the insights you had in the last chapter regarding "thought-labels" and explore the undivided nature of perception at the concrete level of tasting, touching, and hearing. The main point of this section is to awaken you to the fact that experience is not only effortlessly sparkling within you, but that it's not divided between a subject and an object. The basic confusion regarding feeling separate from experience stems largely from our ways of thinking. We do not experience in terms of subjects and objects; we *think* in those terms. When you do not realize this, the grammar of language seems to divide and limit your experience. We say, for instance, "The sun shines," which makes it sound like the sun is a separate entity that does something called "shine." But in reality, there is no sun *apart* from the shining. The sun *is* the shining.

Similarly, your nature as awareness is to shine as thinking, sensing, and perceiving. For example, take the statement, "I see the tree." In the same way that there's no sun apart from shining, there's no "you" apart from seeing. We tend to think that awareness shines *on* things. But as we have seen with the exploration of dream yoga above, that's a mistaken assumption. In fact, awareness is the common source-substance of thinking, sensing, and perceiving. Thinking, sensing, and perceiving *are* awareness. When the sense of conscious presence manifests, awareness spontaneously radiates the boundless totality of experience like the sun radiates rays of light, and just as the sun cannot be divorced from its rays, awareness cannot be divorced from its experiential expressions.

In other words, you don't *see* sights, *hear* sounds, *taste* flavors, *touch* textures, or *smell* fragrances. Seeing *is* the sight; hearing *is* the sound; tasting *is* the flavor; touching *is* the texture; smelling *is* the fragrance. There's no separate person who's experiencing these things. The true "body of experience," therefore, is borderless.

To begin to get in touch with the borderless body of experience, you must "come to your senses"—literally. There's a great quotation by Ludwig Wittgenstein: "The limits of my language mean the limits of my world." Normally, we live within the conceptual limits of language and ignore altogether the actuality of direct sensory experience. When you reverse this tendency and ignore the limits of your language, you find no limits to your world.

Let's explore undivided perception in three guided meditations, which will help you discover that sensing is *inside* you and that there is no division between the subject and object of experience. Although I have only provided meditations for three of your senses, you might consider making up additional meditations for the other senses and applying the same basic approach.

GUIDED MEDITATION: Being the Tasting

For this meditation, you will need something to eat, ideally something you really enjoy, such as a piece of ripe fruit or your favorite chocolate.

1. Once you have your chosen treat, take a moment to soften the system by taking a few deep, conscious breaths.

2. With a relaxed body-mind, take a slow, deliberate bite of your treat. As you do so, become completely absorbed in the tasting so that you are not thinking about anything. You are just *being* the tasting.

3. Now try in your direct experience to separate the "taster" from the "tasted." The "taster" is the thought-label of your conventional name ("John," for example), and the "tasted" is the thought-label for whatever treat you have chosen to eat ("mango," for instance).

4. Now, as you continue being the tasting, try in your direct experience not to separate but simply to *locate* the place where the taster ends and the tasted begins. Can you find a dividing line?

5. Isn't your tasting of the treat inseparable from the treat itself? Aren't they one and the same thing? Isn't there just a boundless experience of tasting?

6. Can you notice that the tasting is *inside* you? If the tasting were "outside" you, would you be aware of it?

7. When you are fully present to and absorbed in it, can you notice that the tasting fills up the *entirety* of your field of experiencing? In that moment, is there anything "outside" it in your experience?

8. Reflect on your experience for a few minutes—and enjoy the rest of your treat!

The point of this meditation is to highlight the fact that both the "taster" and the "tasted" are thought-labels—which constitute the conceptual "limits of your world"—but the "tasting" is an actual experience without limits. Tasting is real. It is concrete. When you try in your direct experience to separate the taster from the tasted or even to *locate* them, you won't be able to do so. You may want to repeat this meditation several times to get the feel of it!

GUIDED MEDITATION: Being the Touching

Let's further explore the undivided nature of perception with the sense of touch.

1. Take a moment to close your eyes and rub your hand back and forth on your leg.

2. Ignore the thought-labels "hand" and "leg" and simply put your full attention on the sensation itself. *Be the touching.*

3. Can you notice that there is just one sensation there?

4. The entire sensation is "yours" because "your" hand is rubbing "your" leg. You are both the subject and the object of the meditation.

5. Now, take your hand and rub it back and forth on the chair. Again, ignore the thought-labels "hand" and "chair" and simply put your full attention on the sensation itself. *Be the touching.*

6. Are there two different sensations there, or is there just one sensation? As you are being the touching, isn't there just one sensation, just like with your hand and leg? What's the difference from the perspective of the sensation itself? Isn't the sensation "yours" in exactly the same way that it was with your hand and leg? Nevertheless, in this part of the meditation, you are likely to consider the object that you are touching "other" than you. But why? Is the sensing itself "other" than you? Experientially, you are both the subject and the object of the experiment as you were with your hand and leg.

As you are being the sensing, you are the single, undivided, borderless experience that you conceptually divide into "you" and something "other" with the use of thought-labels. Again, perform this experiment as many times as it takes to become transfigured by this experiential insight.

GUIDED MEDITATION: Being the Hearing

Let's try the same meditation but with the sense of sound. A Tibetan singing bowl would be ideal. If you don't own a Tibetan singing bowl, you might consider looking for a video, perhaps on YouTube, that has a recording of one. Alternatively, you could do this meditation while listening to a soft, gentle piece of music.

1. Once you have your singing bowl (or piece of music), take a moment to soften the system by taking a few deep, conscious breaths.

2. With a relaxed body-mind, strike the singing bowl (or listen to the music) in a mindful, meditative way. As you do so, become completely absorbed in the hearing so that you are not thinking about anything. You are just *being the hearing.*

3. Now, as you continue to make the sound, try in your direct experience to separate the "hearer" from the "heard." The "hearer" is the thought-label of your conventional name, and the "heard" is the thought-label for the object ("Tibetan singing bowl"). Are you able to separate them, or is there just a single vibrational experience of hearing?

4. When you make the sound, try in your direct experience to locate the place where awareness of the sound ends and the sound itself begins. Can you find a dividing line? Isn't your hearing of the sound inseparable from the sound itself? Aren't they one and the same thing?

5. Isn't hearing taking place *inside* you? If it were "outside" you, would you be aware of it?

6. Reflect on your experience for a few minutes.

In these kinds of meditations, you come to understand and feel how you have been living in the pale world of conceptual thought-labels instead of in the vibrant, boundless reality of conscious experience. Repeated experiments like these will strengthen your experiential insight, generate confidence in your unity and wholeness, and produce in your countenance the beautiful quality of *ziji.*

A Quick Review

You have now finished the second step of the two-step process that began with the "path of negation" and ended with the "path of inclusion." In this chapter, you considered and meditated on how awareness is the boundless source-substance of the entire field of experience. You learned the basics of dream yoga and performed some meditations on the spontaneous, undivided nature of perceiving and sensing. All these pointers were meant to help liberate you of the belief that the world exists independently of awareness, that it's made of something other than awareness, and that you are separate from it. With repeated meditations, you will eventually feel your self as inseparable from the flow of life and your eyes will shine brightly with what Saint John of the Cross calls "a living flame of love."

CHAPTER 9

NON-DUAL SHADOW INTEGRATION

So far, this book has been an invitation to awaken to the inherent perfection and simplicity of your true nature. Now we come to the human dimension, which perhaps not surprisingly complicates matters. While the uncreated reality is dimensionless in an absolute sense, it can be regarded as multidimensional in a relative sense, which gives texture to reality and embraces all levels of your experience. In other words, realizing the perfection of your true nature in an absolute sense doesn't erase the many relative aspects of your being, nor does it eradicate the difficulties and challenges that come with being human. It would not be wise to deny that there is pain, trauma, grief, and heartbreak in the human experience.

In short, you have a shadow, and there's no way to bypass shadow material. Rather, you must integrate it in the light of your awakening. You must learn to have a conscious and intelligent relationship *with* the complicated, shadowy elements of your humanity that will persist beyond your awakening. Shadow material may consist of anything from common triggers and harmless annoyances to deep-seated emotional wounds, addictions, disgust with or aversion to socio-political circumstances, outrage at injustice or abuse, grief, and existential fears associated with sickness and death. It's important to have a nuanced understanding of this complexity in order to honor not only the light, but also the darkness that's part of life. If you do not honor and own your shadow, your light is likely to be either naive or fake.

The goal of this chapter, therefore, is to introduce you to the importance of integrating shadow material rather than bypassing it, to provide you with an overarching paradigm of shadow integration in the context of non-duality, and to alert you to some common misconceptions that people have regarding this path. It is my hope that this broad introduction to non-dual shadow integration will motivate you to work with your own shadows in the next chapter in a way that's maximally evolutionary to your relative humanity within the absolute context of your inherent perfection.

What Is the Shadow?

Throughout this book, we have deconstructed the myth of containment and replaced it with boundless awareness, but the fact of the matter is that even after awakening, the body-mind retains some of the more deeply rooted memories and habits that it has acquired over many years, decades, or even lifetimes of conditioning. I have never met anyone who was exempt from this rule. After awakening, you might wonder what to do with the darkness that remains. The purpose of this chapter and the next is to help you navigate those murky territories.

In Sanskrit, your more deeply embedded memories are referred to as *samskaras* (mental impressions) and *vasanas* (deeply rooted habit patterns or latent tendencies). When you awaken, some of these *samskaras* and *vasanas* will naturally weaken and may even disappear altogether, but some will remain. The key to the approach I'm presenting here is not to "get rid" of them but to learn how to have a conscious, intelligent relationship *with* them. They are part of your humanity, and you simply cannot get rid of your humanity. Furthermore, why would you want to? Conditioning keeps consciousness vigilant and humble in order to safeguard against spiritual ego and pride. Quite simply, conditioning "keeps it real."

The great Swiss psychiatrist Carl Jung used the term "shadow" to refer to all the things in our lives that we have denied, disowned, suppressed, or repressed. Jung speaks with remarkable insight regarding the importance of shadow integration on the path of what he called "individuation," a lifelong process of harmonizing the conscious and the unconscious into a whole, well-functioning personality. There are familial, individual, biological, and collective human shadows, and you will encounter all of them during your awakening and integration. Shadow work requires a willingness to allow the light of awareness to shine in the darkness of whatever has been avoided in your life for whatever reason.

Not only does the shadow not disappear altogether when you awaken to the absolute perspective, but it will appear *more* in awareness as a consequence of your new experiential insight into the nature of reality; in fact, integration becomes an imperative for consciousness after awakening, as it is a process that flows naturally when the egoic defenses fall away. Shadow integration becomes a natural corollary to awakening, therefore, and requires not so much an active doing but a passive, gentle allowing. Development and integration happen organically when the apparently separate self no longer blocks or sabotages it.

I will discuss this technique of allowing in the next chapter. The upshot of this approach is that, when left alone, conditions naturally work themselves out, find relative balance, and self-liberate—just like a physical wound that heals automatically by supremely intelligent though impersonal and non-conceptual natural processes. Awareness heals psychological, emotional, and somatic wounds in the same way that the body heals physical wounds. You can relax in the certainty that you, like all things, are safe and taken care of by a supreme intelligence that knows the way and that wants to heal and integrate if only you will kindly step aside and allow it to do so. There's no separate, contained person who needs to "work it all out." What a relief!

A Synthesis of the Sudden and Gradual Paths

There are two main schools of awakening: the "direct path" schools that emphasize sudden awakening and the "gradual awakening" schools of meditation, yoga, and therapy that emphasize process. The problem with the direct path teachings is that they tend to dismiss integration and development, leaving little or no room for the compassionate embracing and transformation of residual conditioning after awakening. Conversely, the problem with process-oriented systems of awakening and healing is that they tend to strengthen the seeker and are usually blind to the non-progressive reality of non-dual awareness. With progressive paths, you spend your life journeying *toward* the goal of realizing your true nature, trying over many years to remove the obscurations that are apparently blocking your self-realization.

As a starting point, I'm suggesting that you begin from the radically free perspective of "sudden awakening" that I have been pointing to throughout this book rather than from an imaginary starting point of egoic separation. This topsy-turvy approach offers a refreshing alternative to the notion that there's something fundamentally wrong with you, that you are incomplete as you are in this moment, that you have some kind of disorder that you need to "fix," or that you need to journey in space and time to find or be your self. Once it is clear that you have only ever been boundless awareness conceptually imagining yourself as a contained self that changes and develops, the terms "self-development" and "self-help" become less charged and even meaningless. This absolute perspective gives you immense space and frees you up to allow the totality of experiencing to flow through inherently open awareness. In this sense, the individual and universal bodies are brought into harmony and become integrated into an undivided, holistic, fluid field of conscious experiencing.

Then whatever appears, including all the uncomfortable bits, can be allowed from a place of timeless completion. I use the phrase "timeless completion" because, in the awakened state, life does not progress along a line of time, nor is it seeking completion in some future event called "integration" and eventual "death." Life itself doesn't have a lifespan; it is eternal. In the words of a profound Zen saying, "The morning glory which blooms for an hour differs not at heart from the giant pine, which lives for a thousand years." Life itself is timelessly complete, cannot be "improved," and does not increase by living "longer" or decrease by living "shorter." It *is*.

From this perspective, in other words, integration is not a goal-oriented process that seeks "completion." Without a goal in mind, there is no absolute "progress" or "regress," just an intuitive, spontaneous, intelligent response to whatever arises. It entails a timeless awakening to the seamless totality of "inner" and "outer" experiencing. Insofar as integrating the shadow from the position of your true nature makes the work *spontaneous rather than linear*, it does not compare the "results" with previous or anticipated data or with some image you have of saintly perfection, which you will never achieve, I assure you. Rather, it is in the nature of awareness simply to allow whatever arises as an end in itself. In order to avoid judging your progress or regress all the time, *it's best not to self-reflect on your state too much and simply to be the truth of it*. This non-self-referential approach keeps you fresh and safe from self-conscious action and merit, which are really masked and dangerous forms of spiritual pride.

The main point from this absolute perspective is that it's unwise to become *attached* to the idea that you advance by stages or degrees because, at the relative level, conditions are never fully integrated permanently; when integration reaches a relative level of stability, the law of entropy sets in. *You must come to see that, ultimately, whatever you achieve or build up will be lost or will decompose*. The entire process of transformation takes place in you without adding or subtracting anything from your essential nature—just like a dream where nothing is gained or lost in an ultimate sense.

The key to this approach is to remain clear about your primary position as boundless awareness and to work with whatever appears in such a way that it becomes an instrument or servant *of* your true nature rather than an imaginary vehicle *toward* it. If you do not discern between what changes and evolves and what does not, you will spend your life working on a fictitious identity. This work is not about "becoming a better person." It's about being the inherently perfect awareness that you can't *help* being. If you merely work on yourself with a progressive mentality that postpones wholeness to some future date, *you are missing the radiant perfection of things as they are.*

On the other hand—and this is crucial—there are relative processes of unfoldment that would be unwise to deny, and if you do not meet and honor your relative conditioning and the innocent woundedness of your humanity, you will continue to act and react unskillfully and cause suffering despite being awake to the absolute perspective. With an absolute perspective as the overall context, therefore, there's lots of space for relative maturation and for the further exploration of traditional meditative, yogic, and therapeutic modalities. I'm suggesting a fluid, dynamic perspective rather than a dogmatic or fixed one. Otherwise you run the risk of dissociation with non-duality or of a never-ending search with meditative techniques or therapeutic modalities.

As I hope to have illustrated, both the sudden and the gradual paths have their merits. Rather than choosing between them, the approach I present here resides somewhere in between these two polar opposite views. Since both paths actually complement each other, I find that they are more truthful and tactically helpful when viewed with a *both-and* rather than an *either-or* mentality. That way you are not only less likely to become dogmatic or essentialist in your thinking, but more likely to meet and integrate the conditioning in yourself (and others) with intelligence, loving awareness, and compassion.

With this *both-and* perspective, which is open-minded and openhearted, I invite you to apply your experiential insights regarding the path of negation, the path of inclusion, and also the path of therapeutic healing. It's wise and skillful with shadow work to flow between various points of view depending upon the context. In one moment, you may need to call upon your insight that you are the uncreated reality to which nothing ever happens. In another instant, you may need to call upon your insight that all conditions are creative, impersonal, interdependent expressions of boundless awareness and are within you and made out of you. In yet another instant, it may be wise to embrace your psychosomatic wounds in the context of traditional and alternative forms of therapeutic healing. Sometimes you will find yourself integrating all three points of view simultaneously. In the long run, you will meet with and integrate circumstances spontaneously without having to think about it.

With absolute understanding as the foundation and with your earnest, heartfelt commitment to remaining true to yourself as the touchstone, you are truly fulfilled, content, and integrated exactly as you are at every moment while remaining committed to meeting the shadow in a continual gesture of humility. This fluidity of being reveals the timeless quality of life without diminishing your respect for the beauty and nobility of relative transformation and evolution.

Two Common Misconceptions About Awakening

I'd like to alert you to two common misconceptions that people have about what spiritual awakening looks like. Hopefully these suggestions will save you from falling into unnecessary pitfalls as you work with the shadow.

Misconception #1: When I Awaken, I'll Always Feel Good

One of my clients once said something that many people can relate to: "It's painful to be here." This statement is true in general but especially for highly sensitive, empathic people who feel everything. It's just plain honest to admit that this human experience is as much about darkness as it is about light. It's messy and painful by nature. In fact, to be born in time and space is to be in pain. To the best of my knowledge, babies aren't born laughing. What is born is discomfort insofar as the play of opposites, which is what makes experience possible, is pleasant and painful in turn. In fact, when you examine your experience carefully, you come to see that pleasure and pain are interrelated; you cannot have one without the other. Each is dependent on and leads to the other. When you deny that fact and are seduced into trying to grasp onto pleasure to the exclusion of pain, light to the exclusion of darkness, feeling good to the exclusion of feeling bad, or being physically healthy to the exclusion of being physically ill, you are lopsided and even deluded in your understanding. In short, you will lack true wisdom and humility. This, perhaps, is the great lesson and legacy of Jesus' painful death on the cross. The truth is that each of us has a cross to bear in this life. Welcome to being human.

Many people who come to me for spiritual guidance want to escape their pain, which is an innocent request but a naive one that does not recognize the fact that pain is a part of life and that you won't always feel good. The truth is that shadow work, when applied skillfully, does have a palliative effect, and it would be disingenuous to pretend as though you are not fundamentally trying to relieve your suffering. If we're honest, that's what the spiritual path is fundamentally about. The Buddha was clear on this point: "I teach suffering and the cessation of suffering."

But there is a difference between pain and discomfort, on the one hand, and suffering on the other hand. Integration is not about escape from pain and discomfort. It's about welcoming and loving whatever arises. It's about warmth and hospitality. In short, it's about self-love. With this perspective, everything is welcome: the light and the dark parts of you. It's not wise to try to banish any mentally or emotionally painful states that may arise but to welcome them home by listening to them with your full, undivided attention. When having a conversation with your best friend, or when listening to a beautiful piece of music, you do not listen with an ulterior motive but simply for its own sake, because it is good in itself. It's the same in regard to your relationship with shadow material. So I invite you to roll out the red carpet not just for the parts of yourself that you relate to like your most honored guest, but also for those parts of yourself that you have heretofore despised and rejected.

Accepting pain and discomfort as a part of life dispels one of the most persistent misconceptions on the spiritual path having to do with the issue of feeling blissful, good, pleasant, or emotionally expanded. Despite whatever image you might have about what awakening looks like, none of these states are requirements, nor are they a litmus test, for living an awakened life. Since the body-mind is nothing *but* a set of conditions interdependently connected to its environment in an endless network of infinite, untraceable causes and conditions, it will feel comfortable one second and then uncomfortable the next. Like the weather, the state of the body-mind is under the jurisdiction of universal natural laws, which is why it's not ultimately in anyone's control. In fact, the wisdom of experience has taught you that you can count on that. Have you ever felt good or "happy" all the time? Of course not! Don't rely on pleasant states for anything—let alone for your peace.

> The relief from suffering is not in getting rid of discomfort but in getting rid of your desire to get rid of discomfort.

In other words, it's not the pains and discomforts of life that are a problem; it's your *aversion* to them that causes suffering. Life is about the alternation of opposites. True peace is not subject to conditions. The more you learn to soften your concentration on the specific content of consciousness and abide with formless attention as the boundless awareness that remains the same no matter what's showing up, the more your relationship to the inevitable ups and downs of life changes radically and the more the conditions will naturally soften a great deal; the highs will get less high, and the lows will get less low. With this perspective, they will eventually even out. On the other hand, the more acutely you focus on the body-mind and reject any particular state, the more likely you are to suffer the discomfort associated with the stark contrasts between the highs and the lows.

If you are not attached to feeling any particular way, you won't be disappointed—nor will you feel as though you have "lost" your awakening—when the body-mind feels contracted or uncomfortable (such as with illness, which is inevitable). As soon as you realize that you are not *in* the body-mind but that the body-mind is in *you*, the state of the body-mind really doesn't matter all that much—not only because conditions do not affect awareness, but also because *all* conditions (positive, negative, and neutral) are made equally out of the same conscious light. It's not unpleasant thoughts, sensations, and perceptions that cause suffering but the sense that they're happening *to* you and that they "shouldn't" be happening. Why *shouldn't* painful states arise? What's wrong with them? One of the principles of shadow work is that the desire to transform, change, or eradicate negative states is itself a negative state. Conversely, the desire to perpetuate, hold onto, or prolong positive states is also a negative state. Both are causes of suffering.

During the "timeless process" of integration, many "positive" states may appear in your experience—for example, emotional expansion and overflows of love and affection are common expressions of awakening—but *beware of the trap of identifying with these expansive emotional states*. They, too, are awareness, but they are no more exclusively awareness than contracted, uncomfortable, or painful states. Since it's boundless, awareness itself isn't "expansive" or "contracted." Only the conditions of the body, mind, and world contract and expand in a relative sense, not awareness. Since awareness is unconditionally open as the ground of all changing experience, it includes but is not dependent upon all relative contractions and expansions.

I'm not suggesting that you should not care for your body and mind; on the contrary, I have written extensively in this book about the importance of self-care. The overall point I'm making in this section is that it is unwise to become *attached* to pleasant expanded states, including states of "good health." The tendency to become attached to pleasant states arises partly from the fact that all biological organisms have a tendency to avoid unpleasant states and to seek pleasant ones; seeking "good energy" and "perfect health," therefore, can easily become an addiction or an unhealthy fixation. It's wiser to take the best possible care of yourself without becoming dependent on any particular state in order to avoid falling into the trap of seeking one state to the exclusion of the other.

Misconception #2: Thoughts Are My Enemy

Yet another misconception has to do with thoughts. Thoughts get a bad rap in spirituality, but you do not need to get rid of them— not even so-called "negatives" ones. In fact, it's impossible to get rid of thoughts except by way of relative, temporary measures. Thoughts arise like gurgling in your tummy. They are natural for a human being. A quiet mind may be more pleasant, but it's not a requirement for living an awakened life. It's about where you place your *attention*. For this reason I make a distinction between psychological thinking and what I call "thoughting."

"Psychological thinking" is what happens when formless attention collapses onto a train of thoughts and absentmindedly identifies with the thoughts, thereby entering into a literal state of daydreaming. Psychological thinking is an active, compulsive process. It has a grabby, sticky, or quicksand quality. It sucks attention into itself. Of course sometimes thinking is necessary and functional—thinking is a genius when it comes to practical planning—but when it devolves into psychological obsession with the past, present, and future, it becomes unnecessary, dysfunctional, and even harmful.

Once you have used thoughts for practical functioning, you can then shift from practical thinking to "thoughting," which is not problematic. Actually, thoughts by themselves are timeless and weightless—even the so-called "bad" or "disturbing" ones. If you examine them closely, there's nothing really there other than a momentary energetic burst. When they are no longer fed with attention and interest, thoughts appear and disappear quite spontaneously and effortlessly. They glide along like birds in the sky. When they lose their "grabby" and "sticky" quality and are no longer consulted for your identity, they are maximally useful for practical purposes.

EXERCISE: Shifting from Thinking to Thoughting

The difference between thinking and thoughting is an important one, so I would like to end this chapter with a practical exercise to drive this point home experientially. In this exercise, I invite you to select a thought that recurs frequently in your field of attention. Then we'll change your relationship to that thought from a state of identification to one of non-identification.

1. Select a "negative" thought that tends to arise compulsively. Some examples might include thoughts like, *I hate myself,*

I'm a failure, I'm stupid, I'm such a klutz, I'm unlovable, I'm not enlightened yet, and so forth. On the other hand, it could be a "positive" thought, such as *I'm so smart, I'm awakened, I'm spiritual,* or *I'm such a good person.*

2. Once you have selected the thought, allow the thought gently to arise in awareness without identifying with it. Just watch the thought flow across the screen of awareness as though it were a sentence that were scrolling along a TV or computer screen. It's just a sentence made of squiggly lines that has been conditioned to arise in your field of attention; you are not required to identify with it or to believe it.

3. Watch the thought evanesce in your field of attention. If it comes with or triggers a familiar feeling tone, watch the feeling tone evanesce, as well. If the thought or feeling tone feels stuck, move your attention from the thought or feeling to something else, perhaps your left foot, which will likely result in a sense of relief and will allow the thought or feeling to flow. Shifting attention in this way demonstrates that when your attention is not on something, it vanishes from your field of experience. Conversely, when your attention is locked on something, it blooms in your field of experience.

4. When the thought dissolves, recall it again gently. Watch it evanesce again without identifying with it. Again, it's just a sentence made of squiggly lines that has been conditioned to arise in your field of attention.

5. Allow the thought to arise and subside for as many times as it takes for it to discharge, or at least diminish, the psychological and emotional aversion or attachment to it. As you do this, you are shifting from thinking to thoughting.

As you practice this shift over time, the thought will lose its charge and arise less and less frequently. It may even eventually cease to arise altogether. However, even if it does arise, it will not be problematic because you will have changed your relationship to it; its charge will have been neutralized. This is not about "positive thinking" but about freeing you from the attachment to negative, positive, and even neutral thoughts, allowing thoughts to arise without your being identified with any of them.

If you had a hard time doing this particular meditation on demand, you might consider rereading the steps above, absorbing the gist of the meditation, and then applying the pointers the next time a relevant opportunity spontaneously arises to practice this shift from thinking to thoughting.

A Quick Review

In this chapter, we established a broad dialectical paradigm of non-dual shadow integration that honors both the inherent perfection of your true nature and the complexity of your humanity in a relative sense. Hopefully you feel inspired to balance the absolute and relative perspectives of timeless perfection and evolutionary integration. This approach is at once clean and messy, divine and human. We also discussed some common misconceptions that people have on this path about what awakening looks like, particularly in regard to the natural discomforts and contractions of life and to the inevitability of thought activity. We ended with a practical exercise that shifted your experience from thinking to thoughting, which has the power to alleviate or eradicate the aversion or attachment to thoughts. In the next chapter, we'll dive into the specific mechanics of shadow integration in a way that's down-to-earth and practical, giving you an opportunity to begin working with your own shadows intelligently, skillfully, and compassionately.

CHAPTER 10

THE MIRACLE OF ALLOWING

We come now to the specific, concrete techniques that will enable you to meet, honor, and integrate the shadow within the context of the "timeless process" that we discussed in the last chapter. In this chapter, you will learn how to meet any shadow that presents itself. The material in this chapter will ideally help you live more authentically on a day-to-day basis by giving you the tools to work with the inevitable challenges of life. You'll learn how conditioning functions, how to relate to conditioning with the right attitude, how specifically to meet conditioning with macrocosmic spaciousness and microcosmic embodiment, and how to deal practically with any unusual energetic expressions in the body-mind that may arise as a consequence of the integrative process. I will discuss the different components of the technique for working with the shadow separately and then consolidate them into a single exercise later in this chapter that will give you the the skills to meet any shadow that arises in your experience.

Unconscious Suffering

Throughout this book, we have displaced the false psychosomatic center of experience with boundless awareness, which is beyond yet present in and as all experience. But even after awakening, the sensation of the separate self may continue to make "encore appearances" in certain psychosomatic densities that have been conditioned to arise over many years. When these densities arise, even after awakening, the tendency is to self-contract back into a powerful sense of localization and personal identity, especially when certain addictive impulses, core wounds, and traumatic experiences are triggered in the system. These deeply entrenched patterns of self-contraction constitute the shadow. Not meeting the shadow results in what I call "unconscious suffering."

Normally, when the shadow arises, most people do one (or a combination) of three things that constitute the elements of unconscious suffering:

1. **Avoidance**: doing something distracting or numbing in order not to feel the uncomfortable thoughts, sensations, feelings, and emotions

2. **Indulgence**: being identified with, expressing, or wallowing in the uncomfortable thoughts, sensations, feelings, and emotions

3. **Interpretation**: weaving and believing a story about the situation and labeling how you feel with abstract concepts like "depression," "anger," "fear," "desire," and "jealousy"

All three elements of unconscious suffering hinge on the assumption that there is a solid, central "me" to which experience is happening. When that assumption is deconstructed as you've been doing in this book, it becomes clear that no matter how powerful the psychosomatic self may seem, your true self cannot avoid, indulge, or interpret the sensations and densities you experience. Awareness itself is incapable of avoiding, indulging, or interpreting anything; it is the separate self-sense that does these things mainly in the form of thoughts that emerge from and become attached to dense psychosomatic sensations. When the shadow arises, therefore, it's helpful to shift from unconscious suffering to what I call "conscious suffering."

Conscious Suffering

When you know from experience that avoidance, indulgence, and interpretation are not skillful, you are finally ripe for conscious suffering, which is the tactical means by which shadow integration becomes possible.

> Conscious suffering is when you (consciousness) wisely choose the discomfort of not avoiding or indulging the shadow rather than unwisely avoiding or indulging it.

Conscious and unconscious suffering are both uncomfortable; it's just that unconscious suffering is unwise because it's repetitive, and conscious suffering is wise because it's evolutionary. To suffer consciously is a form of self-surrender that purifies the shadowy tendencies in the system and transmutes them into more fluid, light-filled expressions of truth. It is also a form of tolerance or endurance that builds character and produces gravitas in your body-mind's energy field. In fact, conscious suffering gives you the power to transmute the shadowy conditions that *can* be transmuted and the strength wisely to endure the shadowy conditions that *can't* be.

Conscious suffering involves two simultaneous levels:

Macrocosmic level: boundless, loving awareness

Microcosmic level: *feeling* the sensations without avoiding, indulging, or interpreting them

The macrocosmic level is associated with the "path of negation" that we explored in chapters 5 and 6, while the microcosmic level is associated with the "path of inclusion" that we explored in chapters 7 and 8. I work with many people who have focused on one or the other level exclusively and are still suffering as a consequence. When I lead them in the direction that I am suggesting here, they immediately feel relief. Both levels really are necessary for authentic spiritual integration and embodiment. Holding both together is like walking on a tightrope since it requires you not to go too far one way or the other. Leaning too far toward the transcendent macrocosmic level tends toward unhealthy detachment or even dissociation, which is often referred to as "spiritual bypassing," while leaning too far into the conditioned sensations tends toward a sticky, equally unhealthy body-identification. Neither level is wise without the other to balance it out. When you hold them both in unison, you're at once transcendent *and* imminent, awake *and* embodied, transpersonal *and* personal, divine *and* human.

The Flow State

When the macrocosmic and the microcosmic levels are brought together in a unified way of being, a universal flow state emerges. The macrocosmic level that I described above—boundless, loving awareness—displaces the false localized psychosomatic center of experience with unconditional, nonlocal openness. When you relate to experience within this overarching context of impersonal emptiness rather than from the perspective of a localized self, it's much easier to work with any energetic phenomenon that arises, regardless of whether the mind labels it "positive" or "negative" energy.

By its very nature, energy just wants to move and circulate. If it's avoided, indulged, or interpreted in reference to an imaginary psychosomatic center of experience, it will become unconsciously directed and stored in cell memory, waiting for another opportunity to manifest (or "reincarnate") until it's allowed to run its course fully, in which case it will discharge itself and leave the body naturally. This is why the psychosomatic self is mostly experienced as a dense, heavy, localized body. The ego sensation most tangibly manifests itself as acute bodily sensations—primarily a sense of muscular contraction in the head, chest (or solar plexus), and stomach—and an anxious energy that runs through the central nervous system, sending its tentacles throughout the limbs of the body and giving the impression of embodied identity. This energy actually just wants to flow *through* boundless awareness and only persists if it's not allowed to do so or if it bumps up against a false center of experience. If there's a sense that the reactions are happening to "you" rather than just happening impersonally, it's helpful to go back to the path of exclusion, empty yourself out again, and rediscover that you are fundamentally free of thoughts, sensations, and perceptions. The thought or sensation that "you" are the one being affected by conditions is just another conditioned event happening in the interdependent dynamic field of experiencing.

By way of an analogy, a person could walk outside on a windy day and feel that the wind is blowing around him, that it's happening *to* him, but the wind would only be "referring" to someone who was egomaniacal enough to think that. There's no center to the wind! Similarly, the belief and sensation that *life is happening to you* requires a narcissistic state of consciousness that depends upon an altogether nonexistent center of experience. In reality, there's just a universal flow of undivided experiencing with no beginning, middle, or end.

Similarly to the strong wind, when conditioning arises in the body-mind, it's not swirling around a solid, central "you." The umbilical cord to conditions can be cut only with this experiential insight. Until then, it really will feel like the storm is happening *to* you and will feel personal.

Actually, the entire secret to a life of flow is contained in these words: *surrender or suffer.* Those are your only two options in any moment. The sooner you ground the body-mind in the truth of surrender as a way of life rather than living in a self-centered state of resistance to the unpleasant and pursuit of the pleasant, the sooner your life will flow swiftly and smoothly without the sensation of snags or blocks.

All Interpretation Is Misinterpretation

The third element of unconscious suffering, interpretation, usually goes along with one of the other two elements. It's a conceptual overlay to the situation that creates a mental sense of separation between you and the bare events and a sensation of energetic blockage, snag, or frozenness. If you are quietly attentive and observant during these times, you can begin to see that energy—the energy we label "fear," for example—is experienced in the form of *raw energetic sensations* that you may *interpret mentally* as "fear," which freezes a natural flow of energy at the level of conceptual thought. Interpretations are always removed from the facts themselves by virtue of their descriptive approximation.

In other words, when the conditions of the body-mind are agitated or your "buttons are pushed," which is by definition an automatic process outside anyone's control, conditioned energy in its raw form runs through the central nervous system. However, conditioning does not have an inherent label, nor is it inherently good or bad. For example, if there's a sensational density or heaviness in the body-mind, you might be quick to label it "depression" without even being aware that "depression" is an interpretation, and a negative one, of the sensations themselves. If you can suspend your interpretation about the situation and simply allow yourself to feel the raw sensations fully in the body without avoiding, indulging, or interpreting them, the energy will run its course, exhaust itself, and naturally self-liberate. Like flowing water, energy always naturally seeks the path of least resistance and flows on. That is the meaning of the Tao (the Way of life), which could simply be described as the universal flow state without blocks or snags.

Rather than avoiding, indulging, or interpreting whatever conditioning arises in the body-mind, I invite you in the shadow exercise below simply to allow the raw sensations to arise with an overall attitude of surrendered allowing, a gesture that is aligned with the Buddhist teaching about freedom through "non-clinging." With an open gesture of allowing or non-clinging, there's no separate "you" doing anything. When "you" as a separate person are absent, only surrendered allowing or non-clinging remains. When "you" as a separate person are present, only resistance or clinging remains. The sensation of the separate self *is* resistance or clinging to what is; it is the antithesis of the Tao.

Core Wounds and Trauma

Developing the centerless macrocosmic perspective also radically changes your relationship to "core wounds" and "trauma," two loaded terms in psychotherapeutic contexts. Many of the unconscious behavior patterns that keep repeating themselves do tend to signal and revolve around what we call "core wounds," but I would like to make an important distinction here in the context of nondual shadow integration. I don't want to minimize core wounds or be dismissive about how painful they can be when they are triggered; they deserve to be respected and honored. At the same time, it's helpful to develop an alternative perspective on core wounds since that phrase turns out to be something of a misnomer when you awaken to the fact that the actual "core" of experiencing is boundless, formless awareness and not a separate person.

The first thing to consider is that there's really only one "core wound" in the human experience: the belief in and felt sensation of separation. What we normally think of as core wounds are more like "secondary core wounds" because they keep repeating themselves cyclically in relation to the *primary* core wound of separation—what I called "the core psychosomatic trauma" in chapter 3 in regard to the formation of the ego-sense. Secondary core wounds can be thought of as really old "tape loops" that have not been fully experienced and allowed in the light of awareness. Once it is clear that you are boundless, loving awareness itself and not a separate person, you can begin slowly to allow the tapes to loop (just like any other form of conditioning) without avoiding, indulging, or interpreting them. They were "recorded" without your knowledge or consent, and they really have nothing to do with you. When the "golden oldies" are not spun around a fictitious center of experience by the motor of interest and attention, the passive allowing I describe in this chapter enables the loops to wind down on their own over time.

When you begin from the standpoint that there's a "you" who *has* a core wound or who has been traumatized, then you can and will spend decades trying to heal it. You may go to psychotherapy, try various forms of self-development, employ positive thinking, and attend endless transformation seminars and workshops, but something will always seem to be missing. You will always feel wounded if you begin with the assumption of being a separate, contained person who *has* a core wound. Core wounds certainly can't be bypassed, but the credentials of the person to whom the wound appears to refer can be investigated and dismissed.

The crucial thing to realize over and over again is that there's no separate person who's wounded; rather, the sensation of being wounded *is* the sensation of the separate person. This is why I'm encouraging you to begin from the macrocosmic perspective of boundless awareness itself rather than as a person who's *becoming* healed and integrated. The latter has no end because the separate person, being itself an illusion of separation, makes completion impossible.

Formlessness Cannot Be Traumatized

When you awaken to the fact that awareness is formless, your perspective on trauma also changes radically. It is only the self-image that can be imprinted or conditioned in the form of traumatic memories, *not awareness*. Since awareness is formless, it's incapable of being imprinted or conditioned. You can only imprint or condition something that has a form. All relative states of consciousness pass through you without altering or imprinting your formless presence in the least.

> The ultimate healing comes by way of discovering that the core of what you are, boundless awareness, cannot be wounded or traumatized because you have no objective qualities that could be impacted.

At the same time, I want to reiterate the importance of not underestimating the pain and power of trauma and wounding. Like all conditioning, trauma and wounds need to be honored, respected, and embraced in a relative sense. With this overall non-dual approach to shadow integration as the foundation, there's ample room for employing traditional and alternative therapeutic modalities that might help heal your body-mind in a relative sense. Follow your intuition about what's best for you, and seek professional psychotherapeutic care if you are struggling beyond what you are able to cope with.

Having the Right Attitude

In addition to allowing conditions to flow within the macroscopic context of boundless awareness, it's equally important to have the right overall attitude in relation to the microcosmic somatic level of conditioning. What matters most is the love and understanding with which you meet *anything* that arises in your felt experience. When the macroscopic level is coupled with affection and compassion toward yourself in the spirit of the path of inclusion and integration, it becomes a powerful energy of intimate, purifying self-awareness capable of transmuting the shadow in a safe, gentle, healthy way. It is not helpful to develop an uninterested attitude of being dismissively blasé with your own or others' conditioning.

You may have met some people, maybe even non-dual teachers, who give the impression of not caring about anything or anyone, of being uninterested. They "stink of Zen" to use the old saying, and are unapproachable, unenjoyable, or uncomfortable to be around. Of course they don't care about that! Thought can trick you into mistaking emotional aloofness or "witness consciousness" for awakening, but those are divided states of consciousness that keep the messiness of manifestation at bay. If you are numbing out or giving off an energy of not caring, you might not be suffering, but you won't be feeling much of *anything*. You will be like an artificial flower with no fragrance or with the odor of cheap plastic.

Therefore, rather than being aloof or, on the other end of the spectrum, harsh, self-critical, or even mean-spirited toward yourself or others, I encourage you to relate to the arising of anything, but particularly the shadow, with the following attitudes:

Lovingkindness: I call the macrocosmic level "boundless, *loving* awareness" to indicate the importance of relating to conditioning not only with spaciousness, but also with tenderness and lovingkindness—in short, with self-care. Nisargadatta Maharaj used a lovely phrase that applies beautifully in this context: "affectionate awareness." You can think of the "boundless" aspect as the masculine principle and the "loving" or "affectionate" aspect as the feminine principle (by "principle" I mean a universal pattern of life energy rather than a gender norm). *The loving, affectionate dimension of boundless awareness is the compassionate link between the transcendent and immanent aspects of awareness.*

In other words, although awareness is spacious, it is not cold and uncaring like space; it is imbued with a warmth, benevolence, affection, tenderness, and intimacy that pours itself into your felt experience of life. Its most elegant and, in many ways, most beautiful expression arises in the form of pure and simple *kindness*—kindness toward yourself and others. Don't underestimate the immense power of kindness; it sends forth ripples beyond the reaches of where the eye can see. The kinder you are with yourself, the kinder you will naturally be with all of existence. Take a moment to put your hand over your heart; what you feel is not cold and lifeless but throbbing with warmth and life energy. Be kind to your heart, and your heart will be kind to others. This is the true meaning of *ahimsa*, which means "nonviolence." *Ahimsa* is a key virtue in many Indian religions and was the foundation of Gandhi's political and social activism. The fact of the matter is that you cannot be nonviolent with others without first being nonviolent with yourself.

When you are working with the shadow, therefore, think of directing loving awareness like a beam of warm, golden sunlight that bathes your own and other people's bodyminds. When you're feeling stressed out and tense, think of how good and healing it feels to lie on the beach on a warm summer's day; as the body drinks in the sun's rays, the cells wake up and tingle as they absorb the sun's luminous nourishment. Instead of being harsh, coldly detached, or "checked out," I'm suggesting that you shine your warm radiance on whatever arises with an aware sunbeam of lovingkindness. That way, you're wisely *un*attached (rather than coldly *de*tached) but simultaneously willing to participate in life with affection—that is, to feel alive. With boundless, loving awareness as your overall reference point rather than a false psychosomatic self, conditions are free and warmly welcome to be exactly what they are in any given moment.

Softening: This is my word for "surrendering." I have found this simple pointer to be supremely effective in my own life and in my clients' lives. Many of my clients, in fact, report that this one pointer was enough to transform their lives altogether. Think of awareness as soft, undefended, and innocent—like a newborn. Try allowing awareness to kiss the shadow as softly as you would kiss a sleeping baby on the forehead. This softness allows you to develop the capacity to be at ease with the full range of life in all its expressiveness and dynamism. I can tell you from a tremendous amount of experience that softening has miraculous powers and that hardening simply does not work.

Cuddling: Instead of pushing the shadow away, think of relating to the shadow as though you were cuddling with it in a warm bed. It's one thing to cuddle with pleasant states, but you know that you're a true lover when you cuddle equally with painful states. Whenever an unpleasant thought, sensation, feeling, or emotion arises in the body-mind, the tendency for most people is to push it away, to kick it out of bed. However, when you kick something out of bed, it keeps returning and pestering you, begging to be loved. When you pull it closer and cuddle with it, however, you turn your enemy into your lover. The key to cuddling with negative states, like anger and hatred—which have extremely sharp, life-threatening claws—is to soften. I know it sounds counterintuitive, but it works. When you brace against the claws, they dig in. When you soften your defenses and cuddle with them, the lion's claws turn into a puppy's paws.

EXERCISE: Working with the Shadow

Now that we have set the foundation with the macrocosmic and microcosmic levels and have established the right attitudes, I'll now consolidate the basic technique that we have been discussing into a single exercise. Although I have numbered this exercise, you should not follow it in a strictly linear manner since these components are ideally going on simultaneously, although you may first need to work with each component individually to get the hang of it. It's more important that you absorb the gist of this way of being and apply it spontaneously in any given situation. It's important to do this exercise at home alone whenever shadow material arises in your system and also in your daily life so there's a seamless flow between all areas of your life. Get creative with your use of time; for example, you might apply this technique in traffic or in a checkout line at the store.

There are four aspects to the exercise:

1. When the shadow arises in your experience, soften your attention into its formless state by withdrawing it from the specific content (this is the same technique that you learned in the guided meditation on "formless attention" in chapter 5). By doing this, you are shifting into the macrocosmic context of boundless awareness. It's important to shift into the macrocosmic level *as soon as possible* because the sooner you get perspective on a shadow, such as an addictive impulse, the more likely you will be not to avoid it or act it out. It's incredibly difficult at first, but it does become easier with earnest practice.

2. Within this macrocosmic context, passively allow all the conditioned thoughts and sensations to circulate through your body-mind in the form of raw energy. Don't avoid the conditioning by pretending it's not there, don't indulge the conditioning by acting it out, and don't mentally label the conditions arising in you. Simply allow the thoughts to flow and *allow yourself to feel the flow of sensations in your system* within the larger context of boundless awareness.

3. Be gentle, kind, affectionate, and compassionate with yourself. Relax. Soften. Permeate the bodily sensations with the

warm golden sunlight of loving awareness while simultaneously remaining in the state of formless attention.

4.   Sit with the shadow in this way for as long as it takes for it
     to subside.

This technique takes practice, but it is not too difficult to get
the hang of and even to master. Conscious suffering is immediately
liberating in that it provides relief from the deterministic drive to
express something like an emotional reaction or a compulsion, and
it also slowly reconditions the body-mind over a period of time to be
in alignment with truth. In other words, the "timeless process" I'm
describing here is both sudden and evolutionary.

How to Deal with the Aftereffects
of Shadow Work

Once you begin to sit with the shadow in this way, many unusual
energetic phenomena may occur. You might feel dense heaviness in
the body-mind, strong kundalini-type energy in your system, or an
impulse to be physically active. Despite the fact that they can be
alarming, all these states are healthy signs that your energy-body is
being activated and rewired. As long as you're not avoiding or
indulging the energy and are sure to keep a healthy macroscopic
perspective, these states are harmless.

For example, as you are becoming integrated and certain patterns and densities are *imploding*, you might want to sleep for hours,
you may feel extremely asocial, or you may become extremely sensitive to noise and crowds. Because this work initiates a profound
cleansing and healing process at a deep cellular level, it takes a lot of
energy, sometimes resulting in fatigue, energetic flatness, and acute
sensitivity to stimuli. If that happens, rest assured that it's part of the
healing process, signaling that your system is hard at work rewiring

the old circuitry at a subconscious level. Treat it as a wintry season in consciousness; spring is sure to come.

On the other hand, as certain patterns and densities are *exploding*, you might feel lots of excited energy and an impulse to exercise, which is an important signal from the intelligence of the body to shake out the stale or stagnant energies that may have built up over many years of suppression. If that is the case, you might consider doing some somatic-based therapeutic modalities, such as ecstatic dance, Authentic Movement, or even conventional physical exercises, such as running, pushups, or jumping jacks. You may even find yourself spontaneously shaking your hands in the air, clapping, or making unusual movements and gestures as your body releases energy. Sauntering or even playing in nature can be very soothing, healing, and balancing during these times.

Then again, as you are becoming integrated, you may find your body-mind becoming more naturally homeostatic and pleasantly grounded without having to rest or release any excess energy. Every body-mind is different; just follow what feels right to you, trusting the innate intelligence of your system to show you the way. The body is an ancient repository of intuitive, non-conceptual wisdom. We have simply not been taught to notice or trust its wisdom, relying instead on mental knowledge, which is always at least one step removed from life itself.

Traumas, Addictions, and Biological Fears

I want to give you a heads-up about sitting with the more deeply rooted traumas, tendencies, and fears. In the beginning, thoughts and sensations will continue to run strongly, especially if you're dealing with something like childhood trauma, an addictive impulse, or the existential fear of sickness or death. This work is not easy; it is sometimes excruciating. As you allow the raw energy to circulate in your system without avoiding, indulging, or interpreting it, the energy will likely cause a terribly uncomfortable burning sensation in your body-mind, prompting you to want to run for the hills. Rather than being a sign that something is wrong, that means it's working!

It may also give the impression that there's a "you" who's being impacted as a center of experience; this is when it's especially important to balance the microcosmic level with the macrocosmic level, which will neutralize the sensation and soften the sense that it's personal. If you do not introduce the macrocosmic level, you will likely "fall asleep" in your thoughts and sensations and will suffer unconsciously rather than consciously. On the other hand, without the microcosmic level, you run the risk of keeping experience at bay and subtly reifying a sense of "you" who needs to be protected. With this two-faceted perspective, you come to see that you are both indestructible (since there's no falsely created self-centered "you" there to be harmed) *and* innocent (since you won't be wearing the armor of defense).

It can be extremely difficult at first not to identify with certain deeply rooted patterns because they are so unconscious, habitual, unquestioned, or unexamined. They can be subtle and sneaky, especially when dealing with trauma, addictions, and biological fears. Addictions, for example, often run on many years or decades of conditioning, and certain biological programs, such as the drive to find a mate or the fear of illness or bodily death, run on the momentum of millions of years of cell memory—that is, on ancient desires and fears. In fact, these kinds of conditioned patterns have so much momentum that they will "play possum" until the right combination of conditions triggers them in your field of experience; for example, a serious illness or medical diagnosis can reveal huge pockets of fear in the body-mind. This is natural, as all organisms are biologically conditioned at a deep cellular level to survive. It just means that there are still some ancient shadows in the hidden corners of the body-mind that are calling for your loving attention and to be kissed by the wisdom of your awakening.

These kinds of conditions generally feel disgusting, bleak, nebulous, unbearably uncomfortable, and existentially dreadful. They may feel like the revolting, icky equivalent of many eels or worms slithering and writhing over each other in a small, murky pond. The body-mind will do *anything* not to face these feelings, but there is absolutely no way around them. You must feel them fully without avoiding, indulging, or interpreting them while simultaneously remaining awake to the larger context of boundless, loving awareness. As you remain steady with the technique and suffer consciously, you are doing your part to meet the shadow wisely.

Seek Professional Help if You Need It

It's important to seek help from a professional mental health care practitioner if you have a trauma or addiction that is potentially overwhelming or if you are in danger of harming yourself or others. If you have an addiction that is out of control, for instance, you should never feel alone, as there are many wonderful conventional and alternative healthcare professionals working today; in addition to traditional licensed therapists, for example, you might also consider working with a licensed transpersonal therapist who's trained in one or more wisdom traditions. There's an abundance of help out there; don't feel shy or embarrassed about availing yourself of it if you feel that it might benefit you. The work I present here for your consideration will ideally *complement* rather than necessarily replace whatever holistic regimen for health feels right to you.

A Radical Perspective on Old Tendencies

I also want to say something about old tendencies that continue to arise after awakening. Many people feel as though the arising of old tendencies displaces the awakened state, but that is not necessarily true.

> From the perspective of awakening, old tendencies do not displace the awakened state; they arise in it.

This perspective is a radical one. However, I want to be clear that this pointer does not give you permission to act out your old tendencies unconsciously or to hide behind some rationale based on a conceptual understanding of the non-dual teachings, which can lead to some awfully nihilistic and harmful behavior. It's not a "get out of jail free" card. Do your best to remain conscious, but when something like anger or annoyance arises, I suggest that you apologize sincerely to whoever may have been hurt as a result, dust yourself off, and get back on the horse (which is a metaphor for remaining steadfastly committed to awakening and to the evolution of consciousness even when you make relative mistakes). When something like anger or annoyance arises, it's wise to sit with the energy of it in the spirit of the microcosmic perspective in order to meet and integrate it in a healthy way. It's rarely helpful to analyze "why" it arose and never helpful to punish yourself over it. As with all uncomfortable sensations in the body, it is helpful to sit with the energy when it arises as soon as possible, not to analyze it but to acknowledge and integrate that energy into your system rather than ignoring it or pretending it's not there. If the sense of the separate self falls away altogether, you may be able to ignore it, but that is not a healthy strategy in the early stages of awakening because the false self-sense can easily misuse this pointer to substantiate itself at subtle levels.

In other words, if you simply give in to your body-mind's tendencies unconsciously, they will get recorded in the physiology, further strengthen the unconscious behavior patterns, and continue to recycle perhaps for many years or even decades in relation to a self that isn't actually there (perhaps a "spiritual self" that's "beyond it all"). Such is the mechanism of addiction and the calcification of identity. The point is to allow them without avoiding, indulging, or interpreting them—*in which case they are arising in the awakened state.*

Also beware of thoughts like, *I'm boundless awareness, so it doesn't matter what I do,* a red flag that may denote spiritual ego-inflation. When you are willing to allow the raw sensations to reveal themselves fully, another possibility emerges: the possibility of true freedom.

Beware of the Spiritual Superego

Be careful, too, that you don't resist your resistances with a "spiritual superego," a sort of inner censor that neurotically judges how you're feeling and tries to convince you that you "should" not feel a certain way. When you as boundless, loving awareness allow even your resistances without avoiding, indulging, or interpreting them, then you are free of the neurotic guilt associated with how you feel at any given moment; you are free to feel what you feel in the flow state without feeling guilty about it. *In a relative sense, being free means being free to be fully human.* During this "timeless process," you will discover that something miraculous happens when you allow yourself simply to feel whatever you feel: at once you find yourself in your natural state—just like that! Despite how difficult it can be, this simple allowing is literally all it takes to enable your true being to shine.

A Quick Review

In this chapter, you learned the technique for meeting any shadow with love, affection, and intelligence. You learned the art of conscious suffering and the importance of retaining a healthy perspective on conditioning while being willing to feel what you feel without avoiding, indulging, or interpreting it. You also learned how to deal with the arising of unusual energetic phenomena at the somatic level as a consequence of shadow work, and finally, you learned some helpful things to consider as you confront the deepest shadows associated with addictions and the biological fear of sickness and death. As you practice this way of being, you will gain confidence in your ability to meet anything that arises with wisdom, humility, and lovingkindness.

CONCLUSION

Congratulations on having completed the journey of reading this book. It is my sincere hope that you have awakened or are beginning to awaken to your true nature and that you have acquired the tools for meeting and working with the shadow in everyday life. As you continue to mature and evolve in a relative sense, be kind and gentle with yourself. Don't forget to soften, soften, soften. When you meet people who are unkind, remember that they are suffering and that their conditioned behavior is impersonal just like the weather. If you come in contact with an angry person, for instance, try to remember something the Buddha said: "You will not be punished *for* your anger; you will be punished *by* your anger." People who are unkind or angry are already in a hell state. Have compassion for them instead of contempt.

Have compassion for yourself, too, when you inevitably make relative mistakes or find yourself acting or reacting in unskillful ways. As treating yourself well becomes your new default mode, you will find yourself treating the world in general with the same care, respect, and dignity. In fact, rather than producing apathy, the liberation of the false paradoxically improves the world situation since you are not apart from the collective. Your freedom benefits the whole when you realize that you *are* the whole. It's only after you have seen through the illusory nature of "the world" as a separately existing phenomenon that you are truly free to help from the fullness of clarity and insight. When you are submerged in the dream of separation, enmeshed in your subjective views that are tangled up with the very situation to which you object, you can make relative progress at best and may even aggravate the situation. To help the world, you must first see it as a projection. Then you have a healthy perspective to see what needs to be done and your every gesture (or lack thereof) will be beneficial to the whole. I wrote "or lack thereof" because there are times when refraining from activity is wiser and more helpful than engaging in it for the wrong reasons.

When you are empty of the false self, you are full of awareness. Only in non-duality is it a compliment rather than an insult to say about someone, "The lights are on, but nobody's home!" This state of "empty fullness" is the next step for humanity, a natural evolutionary process of transcending egoic identification that is unfolding in human beings all over the world. Stop being mesmerized by the doom and gloom of the mainstream news media and focus, instead, on the boundless possibilities that lie before us. You have infinite potential. After all, the entire universe exists inside you! As we have seen throughout this book, there is absolutely no lack in awareness.

Psychological identification leads to essentialism, tribalism, war, and destruction, but when each one of us awakens, we find ourselves spontaneously in a state of love and compassion. Those are the natural qualities of an awakened being. Then the next step is to translate those qualities to the macrocosmic level, thereby integrating one's awakening with the world at large. That is how we make progress on social, political, and environmental issues. Life is service; service is life. Each of us is called at this precarious time in human history to participate in the wellbeing of our global village. We have run out of time and can no longer afford to anesthetize ourselves with empty consumerism, mindless entertainment, narcissistic self-absorption, and cold-hearted apathy. We are dying and are in need of a spontaneous remission. When we realize that boundless, loving awareness is the eternal foundation of all relative experience, we can truly begin to heal ourselves, the culture, and the environment. Until then, we are lost, confused, bewildered by a cacophony of maniacs. You must not wait for sanity to come to you; you must yourself be the bringer of sanity.

If you are reading this, you are awake to some degree. I invite you to own your awakening and to put it into practice by finding some way to be of service. It doesn't matter how small. With simple being as the foundation, the doing will happen. Only don't block it. Being and becoming are two sides of the same coin.

There are many ways to be of service, and they will depend on your unique abilities and inclinations. You may find yourself working on behalf of a social, political, or environmental cause, or you may find that your calling is to provide the healthiest possible home life for your family. You may find that your awakening enhances your capacity to do what you already do but with more compassion: for example, you might be an awakened teacher, artist, doctor, security guard, or sales clerk. On the other end of the spectrum, you may feel called to live an awakened solitary or even monastic life, which is equally a gift to the human condition. Awakening is consonant with whatever your vocation happens to be.

Whatever your path, may you realize your self as the boundless heart of awareness, and may your light shine brightly in the service of beauty, truth, and goodness.

Michael A. Rodriguez is a spiritual teacher who works with people in meetings, retreats, and private sessions on a full-time basis in the United States and abroad. He holds four academic degrees, including a master's degree in comparative religion from Harvard and a PhD in English literature from Florida State University; taught at the university level for well over a decade; and has lived long-term in two monasteries. Drawing always from his direct experience, Michael illuminates the undivided nature of Life or Consciousness with great clarity and compassion, pointing to reality in a way that is free from dogma, ritual, or adherence to any particular tradition. He draws skillfully from the world's wisdom traditions and also integrates Jungian psychology, literature, music, and art into his work to address the full range of human potential. All his work, including his interviews, can be accessed via his website at www.boundlessawareness.org.

Foreword writer **Joan Tollifson** is author of *Nothing to Grasp, Painting the Sidewalk with Water, Awake in the Heartland,* and *Bare-Bones Meditation.* Tollifson writes and talks with people about the living reality here and now. She has an affinity with both Buddhism and Advaita, but belongs to no formal tradition. Her approach is simple and down-to-earth, pointing beyond concepts and beliefs to the immediacy of direct knowing and being. Tollifson has lived in Northern California; rural New York; Chicago, IL; and Southern Oregon. Her main teacher was Toni Packer, but she spent time with many other teachers as well.

MORE BOOKS for the SPIRITUAL SEEKER

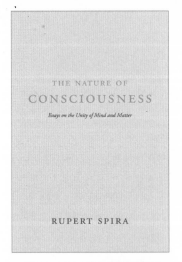
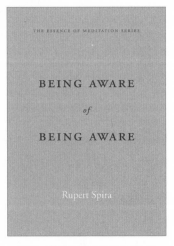
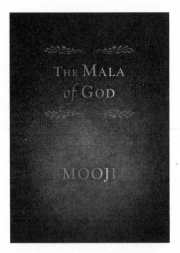